OFFICIAL
SCIENCE FELLOW

YOUR
PHOTO
HERE

P9-DNB-638

CRAZY FOR SCIENCE
WITH
CARMELO
THE SCIENCE FELLOW

CARMELO PIAZZA
and
JAMES BUCKLEY JR.

Illustrated by
CHAD GERAN

Brooklyn, NY

CRAZY FOR SCIENCE

WITH

CARMELO
THE SCIENCE FELLOW

Published by POW!
a division of powerHouse Packaging & Supply, Inc.

Library of Congress Control Number: 2014937050

37 Main Street, Brooklyn, NY 11201-1021
info@POWkidsbooks.com
www.POWkidsbooks.com
www.powerHousebooks.com
www.powerHousepackaging.com

ISBN: 978-1-57687-682-4

Book design: Krzysztof Poluchowicz

10 9 8 7 6 5 4 3 2 1

Printed in Malaysia

CONTENTS

MEET

CARMELO
THE SCIENCE FELLOW

(Not the MARSHMALLOW!)

Hi, my name is Carmelo. I love science! I love it so much that I teach it every day to kids like you. And I love all you banana heads! Wait, what!?

Well, it all started when I first became a teacher and walked into a classroom. The kids were all staring at me as if I had five heads! I wanted to run out! All I could think was, "What in the world am I supposed to do with all these children?" Mrs. O' Dell, the principal, introduced me to the class: "Boys and girls, I would like you to meet Carmelo, your new science teacher." "Ughhh, another boring science teacher," a boy said. "Now, now," said Mrs. O' Dell. "Let's all give Carmelo a chance. Good-bye, Carmelo, and good luck!"

"Oh no," I thought, "now what?!" I decided to just get started. "Good morning, boys and germs," I said. "What?! Germs? We're not germs!" one girl cried out. "Oh, I'm sorry! I meant, Good morning, girls and boggas." "Boggas!" the boys screamed. "This science teacher is weird!" someone whispered. "But he sure is funny," I heard a little girl say. So I decided to keep going. "Well, now that I have your attention,

let's do some science!"

For our first activity, I showed the class how to make ooey-gooey slime. The kids loved it! Nobody thought science was boring anymore! And I loved it, too.

After an hour, I told the kids it was time for the class to come to an end. "Oh, man," said Peter. "Do we have to stop? I'm having so much fun." It was the best thing I had ever heard! And I told them, "Yes, but this is only the beginning. I have a whole bunch of science experiments for us to do! Now, everybody sit on your bum-bum because we are done-done!" Their laughter made me so happy, I couldn't wait to teach again.

I heard later that Peter went home that day and told his dad all about science class. "So, first we took this liquid, and mixed it with another liquid, and stirred, and then took it out and mushed it around till it was …" His dad said, "Whoa, Peter, slow down—I can hardly understand what you are saying. It sounds like you had a great time in science today, but I thought you didn't like science." "Well, now I do!" exclaimed Peter. "We have this awesome new science teacher named Carmelo and he is super-funny and cool." Peter's father replied, "Carmelo is his name? Well, he sure sounds like quite a science fellow!" Peter smiled. "Yeah, Carmelo the Science Fellow."

That night, as Peter was lying in his bed, he kept thinking about science class and what cool things they were going to do next. "Carmelo the Science Fellow," he thought. "I wonder if he likes the color yellow? Hey, that's a funny rhyme; maybe I can make a poem and share it at school tomorrow." He jumped out of bed and grabbed a pencil and paper.

A POEM FOR CARMELO
Carmelo the Science Fellow,
He loves the color yellow,
He eats strawberry Jell-O,
And he's a big fat marshmallow!

When Peter got to school, he showed his friends the poem he had made up. The whole class was laughing. When I got to class that day, I could see that everyone was grinning. "Why are you all so happy?" I asked the class. "We have a poem we made just for you!" said Jenny. "A poem, for me? That sounds really nice." "Okay, you asked for it!" The class burst out in laughter. "What is so funny about a poem?!" I asked. "You'll see." Peter stood up in front of the class. "Okay, guys, let's tell Carmelo our poem." They all began to chant,

CARMELO THE SCIENCE FELLOW,
HE LOVES THE COLOR YELLOW,
HE EATS STRAWBERRY JELL-O . . .

"Stop!" yelled Peter. "So, Carmelo what do you think of the poem, so far?" I had a huge smile on my face. "I think it's awesome!" I said. "Carmelo the Science Fellow—I really like the sound of it!" "Well, there is one more line," said Peter. "I can't wait. I bet it's great!" I replied. "All right, here it goes. Come on, guys," Peter yelled.

AND HE'S A BIG FAT MARSHMALLOW!

The class rolled around in laughter. "WHAT?" I screamed. "The big fat marshmallow!" "Yeah, you're Carmelo, the big fat marshmallow!" they laughed. "What happened to Carmelo the Science Fellow? I liked that!" "No, we like 'big fat marshmallow' better!" the class said. I thought for a minute, and then I said, "Fine, if that's the way it's going to be, then I guess I will just have to call you … a bunch of BANANA HEADS!" "Nooooo, we're not banana heads!" There was laughter throughout the classroom, and I decided from then on that I was going to teach science in a way that made kids laugh like that every day.

So now you know! Whenever I see my students, they say, "Hey, marshmallow!" And I say, "Hiya, banana heads!" I hope I'll get to meet you one day, too—but until then, I wrote this book so you can do some cool science experiments.

And when we do meet, just make sure you say, "Hi, Carmelo the Science Fellow," and not "Hi, marshmallow!"

—Carmelo the Science Fellow

WHAT is AN EXPERIMENT?

As soon as you picked up this book, you became a scientist! An inventor! An engineer! And all you need is a few odds and ends and gear, a bit of help from a grown-up, and your own imagination. This book is going to introduce you to the **scientific method**, which is the process that scientists use to learn about the world around us. The scientific method has been used by creative and curious people for thousands of years to find the answers to their questions about how things work. Here's how you do it:

1 ASK A QUESTION

Scientists always start with a question. Is there something you want to know more about? Are there things in your home, neighborhood, or school that you are curious about? Anything that you are interested in is a good subject to think of questions about. Remember, there are no wrong questions to ask.

2 MAKE A PREDICTION

Before you do anything else, put your brain to work. Just think about your question. Don't try anything or look anything up—just think. Now, what do you THINK the answer to your question is? Use what you already know to guess what might happen—this is called making a **prediction**, which is just a fancy word for a guess. Scientists do this all the time. Guesses aren't wrong (or right) . . . until you prove them wrong (or right!).

3 TEST IT

Now comes the fun part: testing to find out what happens. The tests you do in science are **experiments**. In this book, there are lots of experiments you can do on your own (okay, maybe your favorite grown-up can help) using stuff from around your house. Try them out, following each one step-by-step to see what happens. Sometimes you'll have guessed right, sometimes you won't have. That's okay! Finding out what is true is what makes it science. And, sometimes, unexpected results lead to huge leaps in knowledge!

4 GET YOUR RESULTS

Write down your observations. What did your experiment show? Did it show you a whole different answer than you were expecting? Write down your question, your predictions, and your results—now you have a scientific journal!

WHAT IS TRIAL AND ERROR?

Even simple activities can teach us how to observe and find out how things work. The activities in this book are designed to lead you through a very important scientific process called TRIAL AND ERROR, which means asking questions and then figuring out ways to find the answers—and we keep trying till we have answers that work every time! This way we find out for ourselves how the world works, rather than just reading about it. All branches of science use the scientific method, and in this book, we are going to use it to explore aspects of biology, chemistry, physics, and more.

THE SAFETY TALK

Okay, I have to say this stuff because I'm a teacher and a parent. Be careful! Science can be messy, sticky, gooey, and sometimes even smelly. To do it safely, just follow the steps in this book. Don't eat things you are not told to eat, or drink things you are not told to drink. (There are things in here to eat...I'll let you know which!) And remember, a good scientist always cleans up afterward.

GROWN-UPS: READ THIS!

The experiments and activities in this book are designed so that kids can do nearly everything by themselves. However, you can help by being nearby to help with measurements, assist small hands with pouring or mixing, or to wipe away a tear or a mess after something spills (and it probably will!). Avoid the temptation to dive in there yourself and get your hands messy. Kids will get much more of these experiments if they are truly hands-on; nothing teaches better than doing, and this book is all about DOING, not watching someone else do it. Thanks for sharing your love of science and of trying new things . . . now stand by to help if needed!

CHAPTER 1

THE INVENTION CONVENTION

Unless it grew in nature, just about everything was invented. Someone (or several someones) had an idea . . . experimented . . . and came up with new things or new ways to do things. In this chapter, YOU get to be the inventor! And remember the inventor's motto:

"If at first you don't succeed, try, try again. But make sure to clean up afterward."

Even inventors have moms, after all.

They say that necessity is the mother of invention. I'd just like to mention that Josephine is the mother of Carmelo. I promised that she'd be in the book.

Thomas Edison said, "Genius is one percent inspiration, and 99 percent perspiration." Since perspiration is sweat, that's actually pretty gross.

No, you can't invent a machine that will do your homework for you!

9

POP GOES THE BRAIN!

DO NOT FEAR, BE A SKULL ENGINEER!

Reach up and grab your head. Feel that? No, not your hair. And take off that hat in the house! Now . . . try again. Feel what's underneath your hair and skin? That's your skull! The bones of your skull are super-hard so they can protect your brain. Your brain is the most important part of your body, so you gotta keep it safe! (That's why you wear a helmet when you're biking, scooting, snowboarding, or doing any activity that might involve falling on your head . . . that's a time to keep it extra-safe!) If something whacks your head, your skull is what protects your brain from getting hurt.

In this experiment, you're going to invent a skull. Then we'll smash it against a wall! (Don't worry. Smashing something is okay when it's a key part of an experiment.) Along with the materials to make your new skull, you'll be using one other big piece of gear: your actual brain! Your brain will give you ideas on how to make the skull. Then your brain will tell your eyes and hands how to build it. Having a brain is pretty cool, right?

SCIENCE QUESTION:

Can you make a skull that would protect your brain?

WHY DID THE SKELETON CHASE THE SKULL? It wanted to get ahead!

STUFF YOU NEED
- Balloons
- A pile of stuff from around your house, such as:
  - Pieces of Styrofoam
  - Cups
  - Wrapping paper
  - Cotton
  - Old socks
  - Felt
  - Egg cartons
  - Bubble wrap
  - Newspaper
  - Tape . . . lots of tape!

STEP by STEP

The biggest dinosaur skull ever found was eight feet (2.4 m) long. It was from a torosaurus. Good luck finding a hat that fits that head!

1 **FILL A BALLOON WITH WATER.** If you need help tying the balloon tightly, ask one of those people who used to be kids (you know . . . grown-ups!) Okay, from now on, this water balloon is your brain! How can you keep it from breaking?

REAL-WORLD SCIENCE!

Your skull feels like one big bone, doesn't it? Guess what? **Your skull is actually made up of more than 20 bones!** The hard, round part on top is formed by four larger pieces that fit together like the parts of a jigsaw puzzle. Be sure you don't lose any pieces!

2 Now you're going to **INVENT A SKULL** to hold and protect your balloon-brain. You can use any of the materials you've gathered. (Don't be afraid to try some that are not on my list.) Don't buy any materials . . . be creative! Just use the stuff you find around your house.

3 **BUILD THE SKULL AROUND YOUR BALLOON-BRAIN.** It should surround the entire balloon-brain, ready to protect it from harm! Think about combining hard and soft materials. When you think your skull is well protected . . .

4 **. . . THROW IT AGAINST A WALL!** Yep, it's testing time here at Skull Central. (Quick tip: To avoid a giant mess, do your testing outside. You'll thank me later.) Find a blank wall—pick one that doesn't have anything on it that you could damage. Now stand a few feet away from the wall and toss the skull-covered balloon at it. Aim for the lower part of the wall.

Burst your balloon? No worries! Science is all about trial and error. That means, if it doesn't work, try again!

5 If your balloon does not pop, you saved your brain! **YOU ARE NOW A SKULL INVENTOR!** If your balloon pops, clean up the mess . . . and then it's back to the drawing board! Scientists always learn from their mistakes!

Duh! LET'S PLAY with DOUGH

WHAT DOES A DOUGH INVENTOR SING?
Dough, play, me!

SCIENCE ACTIVITY:

Make your own modeling dough.

You could go to the store and buy some Play-Doh. But you're a scientist now! You can make it yourself and decide exactly how you want it to be—how thick it is, what color it will be, and what you want to do with it! Did you know that the popular squishy stuff was invented by accident? One day back in the 1950s, a guy named Noah McVicker made a product to clean wallpaper. His nephew Joe found out that kids were using the gooey stuff to make models, and the McVickers started selling it as Play-Doh! Way more fun! Velcro, the microwave oven, and even potato chips were also accidental inventions. For this experiment, we are going to make like the McVickers! (Good news, parental units: This dough is nontoxic . . . and edible!)

STUFF YOU NEED

- 1 cup (120 g) flour
- 1/4 cup (60 mL) salt
- 1 tablespoon (15mL) corn oil
- 1 8-ounce (240 mL) paper cup
- Food coloring (if you want your dough to be colored)
- Towels for cleaning up
- Stick or spoon for stirring

SALT

STEP by STEP

Need to knead? Try using your knuckles and palms as well as your fingers.

1 MIX THE FLOUR AND SALT VERY WELL IN A BOWL. Add the oil and stir the mixture again.

2 If you want to make the dough colored, ADD 5 DROPS OF FOOD COLORING to the water.

3 IT'S TIME TO ADD THE WATER. Stir it in a bit at a time—not all at once! (Too much water will make your dough too wet and too sticky!)

4 KEEP ADDING A BIT OF WATER until your mixture becomes thick and feels ready to mold.

5 Take it out and KNEAD IT ON THE TABLE. Once the mixture has the consistency you want for modeling, you're a McVicker … er, an inventor!

6 Now have fun! MAKE A GIRAFFE OR A DINOSAUR OR A ROBOT … make a fossil impression with it … or seal it in a plastic bag and sell it! Cha ching!

CELEBRATE!

Make this stuff on September 16 and celebrate National Play-Doh Day! Making Play-Doh turned out well for the McVickers. They were selling millions of dollars' worth of Play-Doh within a couple of years. Not bad for an accident!

PROTECT THE EGG

Your egg made it through safely? EGG-cellent! EGG-strordinary! What a great EGG-speriment!

Have you heard the expression "what goes up, must come down"? The reason that's true is a force called **GRAVITY**. Huh? Basically, gravity is a force that causes stuff to be attracted to other stuff! It gives everything on planet Earth weight. What happens if you lift something up, then drop it? I bet you can guess. That's gravity in action. The bigger and heavier the item, the more weight it has. When the space shuttle (very heavy) was flying, it needed the push of a rocket to help it leave Earth—it had to escape the pull of gravity. When the space shuttle was landing again, it was gravity that was pulling it home to Earth. Have you ever wondered how it got down safely? And what happens with something lighter— oh, say, an egg? Let's find out!

SCIENCE QUESTION:

Can you make a protective device that stops an egg from breaking?

Remember, it takes a lot of broken eggs to make a great omelet! Keep trying!

STUFF YOU NEED
- Hard-boiled egg (or several)
- Paper towels
- Tape
- Scissors
- Cardboard
- String

STEP by STEP

"Imagination is more important than knowledge."
—Albert Einstein, a really famous scientist

REAL-WORLD SCIENCE!

Here are five awesome space shuttle facts:

— *Columbia* was the first space shuttle. It lifted off—and returned!—in 1981.

—The space shuttle was 122 feet (36.6 m) long—as long as three full school buses!

—One shuttle equals more than 13 elephants—in weight!

—*Atlantis* made the final space shuttle flight in 2011.

—On Earth, the space shuttle rode piggyback on a converted 747 airplane!

1 Your challenge today is to experience gravity by sending your own space shuttle to Earth—safely! Since the space shuttle can't fit into your kitchen, let's use an egg instead. **CAN YOU HELP IT LAND WITHOUT GETTING CRACKED?**

2 Think: How can you protect your hard-boiled shuttle, er . . . egg, as it experiences gravity? Using only paper towels, paper, tape, scissors, string, and other household materials, **CREATE A CONTRAPTION TO PROTECT THE EGG.** Can your contraption make the egg fall more slowly? Does a slower fall save the egg? Would padding help protect it from the impact when it hits the ground?

3 Build your contraption and see what happens when you **DROP THE EGG FROM A CHAIR OR A TABLE** or even from the top of a jungle gym at the playground! How did gravity affect your contraption? What caused your egg to fall more slowly or quickly to the ground? Did padding help to protect it?

4 Remember, science is about trial and error. **IF YOUR EGG CRACKS, DO NOT GIVE UP.** Learn from your mistakes, and design a different device.

NO WAY! YES WAY!

After it landed, the space shuttle was going so fast that brakes alone would not stop it. The shuttle shot out huge parachutes from the back. They helped the speeding shuttle roll to a safe stop.

15

YOU SEE IT,
YOU DON'T

THE INVENTION CONVENTION

DID YOU KNOW?

The stuff inside your pencil is a mineral called graphite. A lar[ge] deposit of **graphite** w[as] found in England in th[e] 1500s, and soon after, the first wooden penc[ils] were made.

SCIENCE ACTIVITY:

Write a note with invisible "ink."

STUFF YOU NEED
- Whole milk (make sure it's not half milk . . . get it?)
- A glass for the milk
- Paper to write on
- Cotton swabs for dipping
- Pencils for revealing (you'll see . . . really!)
- A friend (for reading)

Stuck behind enemy lines and need to send a secret note to your friend? Want to hide your latest great joke from rival comics? How about amazing your friends with your scientific kung-fu? Now you can do all of these things! I'm going to show you how to make invisible ink! (Note: I did not use invisible ink to write this book. Otherwise, you would not be able to read it. I used visible ink. But that's for another lesson . . .)

NO WAY!
YES WAY!

This experiment won't work with other kinds of milk. Why not? With low-fat or skim milk, the fat is nearly all removed. If you used those, it would almost be like putting water on the paper. There would be no fat for the "ink" to stick to!

WHOLE MILK

WHOLE MILK

STEP by STEP

1 Pour yourself a glass of milk. Dip your cotton swab into the milk. Use the cotton swab like a pen, and WRITE A MESSAGE ON THE PAPER. If the tip runs dry, dip again and finish writing!

2 Now TAKE THE PAPER AND GENTLY WAVE IT THROUGH THE AIR. As you do, the milk will evaporate. The paper is blank . . . or is it? Bwa-ha-ha! (Sorry, that was my mad scientist coming out . . . I'm better now.)

REAL-WORLD SCIENCE!

Spies in World War II used a different sort of invisible ink made from lemon juice. They wrote on paper with the ink, and then they sent it to their bosses. The bosses held the paper over heat . . . and the message appeared!

3 The water has evaporated, but THE FAT FROM THE MILK IS STILL THERE on the paper. You need something to stick to the fat. This will reveal your hidden message.

4 Here's the cool part: Take two pencils and RUB THE TIPS OF THE PENCILS TOGETHER. Do this while holding the pencils above your hidden message. It will look like black snow or pepper is falling. That's the graphite from the pencils, forming a kind of powder.

5 Now take your pointer finger and gently RUB THE GRAPHITE POWDER ACROSS THE NOTE. The graphite will stick to the fat from the milk. Your message will appear like magic!

6 Now you need that friend so you can SHOW OFF!

CAN PLAY CLAY MAKE BOAT FLOAT?

The great boxer Muhammad Ali was born Cassius Clay. That has nothing to do with floating boats, but he was pretty awesome!

SCIENCE QUESTION:

Can you make a shape that floats?

REAL-WORLD SCIENCE!

Clay is one thing . . . concrete is another! Every year, college engineering students can enter a concrete canoe race. They have to make a boat out of concrete and then race it against other students! Yes . . . boats made of concrete really float!

Here's an experiment you can do with the dough you made a few pages ago. Make a ball of it and put it in a pan of water. What happens? That's right. It flies into the air and zooms around the room. Pretty cool, right? No? That didn't happen? It sank? Okay, forget what I said about the flying part. I was confused! Just kidding . . . I knew it would sink. But now you, your brain, and your hands will make it float. The key is the shape you make. Take your ball of clay and test a series of different shapes. The only rule is that you are not allowed to use a smaller piece of clay. You must use the entire ball of clay and get it to float.

STUFF YOU NEED

- Clay or homemade modeling dough (see page 12)
- A container of water
- Some paper towels
- Pennies (I'll explain later)

One of the heaviest ships in the world (they're always building new ones!) was the *Seawise Giant*. It weighted more than 1.2 million pounds (almost half a million kilograms) —and it floated!

Do you know what happens when snack-size Snickers and Three Musketeers Bars are placed in water? Test it and then eat your results. LOL!

1 TAKE THAT BALL OF CLAY AND MOLD IT INTO A DIFFERENT SHAPE. What shapes can you try? What can you do to the ball of clay to try to get it to float?

2 Do you think a worm shape will float? How about a flat pancake shape? Maybe a U shape? Remember, the key is to ask a question, make a prediction, test it, and write down your results. DID ANY OF YOUR SHAPES RESULT IN A FLOATING BOAT?

3 Okay, you did it! You made a clay boat. Way to go. Now, we'll see how good your boat really is. TIME TO LOAD IT UP! Add passengers to your boat. (Note: Please do not start adding your friends or little brothers and sisters to the boat! Thank you.) Put the pennies on board one at a time to see how many passengers your boat can hold. What's your limit? Can you try another shape to hold MORE pennies? Try a boat challenge with your friends!

THANKS, GREEK DUDE!

A Greek scientist named **Archimedes** (ark-uh-MEE-deez) discovered why boats float when he was taking a bath! When he got in, the water sloshed over the sides, and he realized that his body was taking up the space where the water was, or "displacing" it. He shouted "Eureka!" which means "I found it!" in Greek. His discovery helps engineers today create new boats and boat shapes.

THE INVENTION CONVENTION

Can you make a rocket "ship" that is powered by nothing but air?

THE ROCKET BALLOON "SHIP"

Newton came up with the theory of gravity after watching an apple fall from a tree.

In your last activity, you experimented with one material—clay—and realized that the same substance can both sink and float. The changes you made to the shape made the clay float. There are some materials, however, that float all the time. If you don't believe me, try testing a piece of wood, cork, or even an ice cube. It's true: they all float! In this next experiment, the first thing you are going to do is make a floating "ship." Then you are going to see if you can make it move forward using nothing but air! How is this possible?

Let's find out! Have you ever heard of a guy named Sir Isaac Newton (1643–1727)? He was a British scientist who studied math and physics. Newton's Three Laws of Motion explain how objects move. In this experiment, you're going to discover Newton's Third Law of Motion, which states that for every force, there is an equal and opposite force. A **force** is something that pushes or pulls. In this case, as the air rushes backward out of the balloon, it pushes the ship forward in the opposite direction with an equal amount of force. Your job is to make the most of this force!

REAL-WORLD SCIENCE!

NEWTON'S LAWS

FIRST LAW: Stuff stays where it is unless you move it. Stuff that's moving won't stop until you stop it. Impress your friends by calling this by its fancy name—**inertia** (in-ER-shah).

SECOND LAW: The bigger it is, the more force you need to move it. This is also known as "duh!" law. No, not really. He was actually pretty smart to come up with this one.

THIRD LAW: See above!

STUFF YOU NEED
- Styrofoam plate
- Flexible straw
- Balloon
- Tape

1 Okay, go through your house and FIND A STYROFOAM PLATE. Just like objects made of wood or cork, this plate will always float. (This is the easy part of this experiment.)

2 Your challenge now is to build a ship out of this Styrofoam plate. START BY CHOOSING A COOL SHAPE FOR YOUR BOAT and cut it from the plate.

3 Take your balloon, BLOW IT UP, AND THEN LET ALL THE AIR OUT. This will make the balloon easier to blow up again later.

4 TAKE THE OPENING OF THE BALLOON AND TAPE IT AROUND THE SHORT END OF THE FLEXIBLE STRAW so that no air can escape; you will be able to blow up the balloon by blowing into the straw.

5 TAPE THE LONG END OF THE STRAW DOWN TO THE CENTER OF YOUR BOAT with the open tip of the straw hanging off of the plate. You will need to leave enough of the straw's tip off the edge so that you can blow up the balloon.

6 Take your boat to the bathtub. RUN THE WATER until the tub is about a third full.

7 BLOW UP YOUR BALLOON through the straw and then pinch the end of the straw closed. Place it on the water, let go of the end of the straw, and see what happens!

8 DID YOUR BOAT ZOOM OFF LIKE A ROCKET? Blow up the balloon and do it again!

9 When the air comes out of the balloon, which direction is moving—away from the balloon? WHAT DIRECTION DOES THE ROCKET "SHIP" MOVE?

CHAPTER 2

YOU, ME, AND BIOLOGY

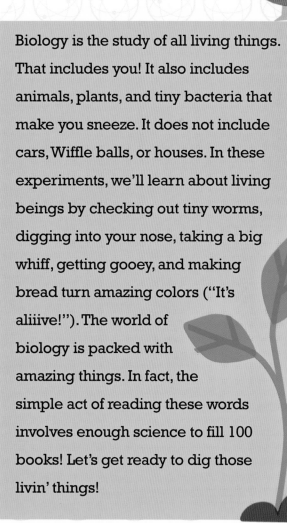

Biology is the study of all living things. That includes you! It also includes animals, plants, and tiny bacteria that make you sneeze. It does not include cars, Wiffle balls, or houses. In these experiments, we'll learn about living beings by checking out tiny worms, digging into your nose, taking a big whiff, getting gooey, and making bread turn amazing colors ("It's aliiive!"). The world of biology is packed with amazing things. In fact, the simple act of reading these words involves enough science to fill 100 books! Let's get ready to dig those livin' things!

Do you know what makes Earth the coolest planet in the universe? We have life! As of now, Earth is the only planet that we know of that has living things. Not only do we have life on planet Earth, we have **biodiversity**. That means we have a lot of different plants, animals, and other species in a particular habitat at a particular time. To understand why biodiversity is important, we have to think like biologists. If planet Earth is the only planet with life, we really want to try and keep it this way. Let's become biologists, and study some of Earth's most amazing creatures.

IMPRESS YOUR PARENTS

The word **BIOLOGY** is from ancient Greek. **"Bio"** means life and **"ology"** means "the study of."

Do you know any other "ology" words? Here are some of my favorites (and a few I made up)—can you guess what subjects these "-ology" words are about? Do you know which ones are real? Look them up to find out if you were right.

Now, can you think up a few of your own?

WORD	PREDICTION	DEFINITION
Bubbleology		
Geology		
Ecology		
Fartology		
Archeology		
Futurology		
Boogerology		
your -ology word goes here		
your -ology word goes here		

IN THIS CHAPTER:

MIGHTY MORPHIN' MEALWORM!

SCIENCE ACTIVITY:

Observe a change.

Caterpillars get a lot of attention when they change into butterflies. But caterpillars are not the only creatures who make big changes on their way from baby to big kid! With the help of the mighty mealworm, we're going to observe an amazing (take a deep breath!) **METAMORPHOSIS**!

The very long word means "change." (So why don't we just say "change"? Because scientists LOVE big words!) An animal that goes through metamorphosis ends up with a very different body than the one it starts out with. Let's watch!

Mealworms are used as food for many pets, including reptiles, birds, and fish. Would you eat a mealworm burger?! Ewww! Scientists in the Netherlands found that raising mealworms used far less energy than raising cows. They suggested that people could start eating mealworms as a great source of protein for less cost. Yes, you can use a lot of ketchup!

STUFF YOU NEED
- Mealworm—duh! (Pet stores usually have mealworms to sell as food for other pets)
- Paper cup or empty left over takeout food container
- Oats
- Apple
- Aluminum foil
- Rubber bands

IS THAT AN INSECT?

Insects have three body parts: a head, thorax, and abdomen. Mealworms don't. So is the mealworm an insect? Check out what it becomes and then decide.

1 First, **OBSERVE YOUR MEALWORM.** You can touch it, feel it, hold it, and even kiss it. (Gross!) If you are afraid to touch it, then use a toothpick to gently pick it up. What color is it? How long is it? How does it feel? Draw a picture or write down what you see.

2 Now **MAKE YOUR MEALWORM A HOME.** A paper cup or clean, empty plastic food container will do. Fill up the cup with dry oats (not cooked oatmeal . . . they hate that!). The mealworm will eat and live in the oats. Add a slice of apple or a piece of potato. Mealworms can get water from them. Cover the top of the container with foil and secure it with a rubber band.

3 More observing time: **REMOVE THE FOIL EACH DAY AND PEER IN.** Did the mealworm eat? Did it drink? Record what it does every day in its home. How does it change over time?

4 Soon, something really cool will happen. **YOUR MEALWORM IS GOING TO START LOOKING LIKE A MUMMY.** Its color is going to change. Its body is going to start morphing (changing). What is happening to your mealworm?

5 After a few weeks, the mealworm will be gone. Is it dead? Did it move to Hawaii? Is it living in your sister's hair? No, **IT WENT THROUGH AN AMAZING METAMORPHOSIS** and turned into a darkling beetle! (Note: Do not put the beetle in your sister's hair.)

ANSWER

Now that it's grown up, you can see that the mealworm is an insect!

YOU, ME, AND BIOLOGY

25

HOORAY FOR BOOGERS!

Don't stop with green! Try other colors so that you have a rainbow of boogers!

It's a bird, it's a plane, it's SUPER-BOOGER! I picked this experiment carefully (get it?!) because I just "nose" that you'll have fun with it. Don't worry, it's "snot" hard! Ha ... sorry, I got carried away. Boogers are certainly gross, but they are also important. Boogers are the human body's superheroes. They trap germs in their sticky goo, so that you can sneeze or blow them out. When we are sick, the boogers are greener because they trapped more germs. In fact, without boogers ... we might die! So let's make some and see how they work!

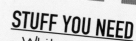

STUFF YOU NEED
- White glue
- Water
- Borax powder (find this in the laundry section of the grocery store)
- Food coloring
- 16-ounce (80 mL) empty plastic bottle
- Cups
- Craft sticks
- Bags

WHAT'S THE DIFFERENCE BETWEEN BOOGERS AND BROCCOLI?
Kids don't eat broccoli.

WHY DID THE MAN CATCH HIS NOSE?
Because it was running.

1 Get a grown-up to help. PUT ABOUT 10 TEASPOONS (50 ML) OF THE POWDER IN THE EMPTY WATER BOTTLE.

2 ADD WARM WATER so that the bottle is just about full. Shake the bottle for about one minute.

3 When you stop shaking the bottle, you are going to see that SOME OF THE BORAX POWDER DID NOT DISSOLVE and has settled to the bottom. This is perfect. You have now created something called a SATURATED SOLUTION.

In an empty cup, PUT 4 TEASPOONS (20 ML) OF WHITE GLUE AND THEN ADD 4 TEASPOONS (20 ML) WATER. Use the craft stick to stir this around so that you have a glue-and-water mixture.

5 ADD 2 TO 3 DROPS OF GREEN FOOD COLORING and stir so that you now have a green mixture.

6 Add one bottle cap of the borax solution to the green glue-and-water mixture. Stir it around and then pull out the stick. What do you see? Some of the liquid has turned into something new that was not there before. IT'S A BOOGER!!!

7 There is still liquid left over, so please add another capful of borax. Stir again, and you are going to notice that your booger grew in size. Keep going: Add another capful of borax solution. KEEP ADDING CAPFULS OF BORAX SOLUTION until there is no liquid left in the cup.

8 Here comes the fun part: Once your reaction is complete, and all of the liquid in your cup has turned into this fun slime, PUT YOUR HAND IN THE CUP AND TAKE OUT YOUR SLIMY BOOGER. Roll it around your hand until the mixture is no longer wet. Make sure you press it, roll it, knead it, and keep on doing it. Your artificial booger is done!

9 Now it's time to TEST YOUR BOOGER. Walk around the room and touch the booger to different surfaces, like the floor or the table. (Not the good furniture! No, not the dog, either!)

10 IS YOUR BOOGER CATCHING STUFF? What kinds of things do you see in it? Imagine the boogers in your nose doing the same thing—what might they catch?

YOU, ME, AND BIOLOGY

WHAT IS THE SHARPEST THING IN THE WORLD?
A fart. It goes through your pants and doesn't even leave a hole.

YES. IT WAS ME!

Some of the things that our bodies do are, I have to admit, kinda gross. We're talkin' boogers, earwax, sweat . . . eeew. All of these have a purpose, though, which is to help us stay healthy. And then there's farting! Okay, stop laughing . . . this is science! Farts happen when your body builds up gas inside . . . and the gas has to come out! Brrrappp! It's not me, Mom . . . it's my gas! In this experiment, you're going to make a fart bag. You'll be able to create fart after fart . . . without having to eat a lot of beans! You'll be able to say, "Yes, that was my fart. And I'm proud of it!"

SCIENCE QUESTION:
What causes a fart?

STUFF YOU NEED
- 1/2 cup (120 mL) white vinegar
- 1 1/2 tablespoons (25 mL) baking soda
- Paper towels
- Zipper-lock bags
- Measuring cup
- Tape
- Spoons

DID I DRINK GASOLINE?

No, the type of gas that makes farts is not like the gas you put in a car. The gas in your stomach is created when your body digests food. It is like air, but it can be smelly. (Gasoline is not actually even a gas; it's a liquid.)

CARMELO'S OWN FART STORY

When I was 13 years old, I had to have my appendix removed. I was in the hospital for days. I kept asking the doctor, "Can I go home now?" and each time, he would say, "Have you farted?" I cracked up, and said, "Seriously, doc?" "I am serious! Have you farted?" He explained to me that after an operation like the one I had, patients have to stay in the hospital until doctors are sure the patient's system is working properly. The best way to tell that is if the patient can fart successfully! So when I farted, I got to go home. And now, I know farting is a sign of good health!

STEP by STEP

A skeleton was trying to fart in a crowded place. But in the end it couldn't, 'cause it had no guts.

1 This could be messy, so the first step is to FIND A SPOT to do this experiment where a mess is okay—you can even do it outdoors.

2 It's very important to USE A BAG WITHOUT HOLES. To test a zipper-lock bag, pour water in it. Zip it closed and turn it upside down. If no water leaks out, you can use that bag. Unzip it and pour out the water. If the bag leaks, try another one. Keep testing bags until you find one that doesn't leak.

3 Now MAKE A TIME-RELEASE PACKET. Tear a paper towel into a square that measures about 5 inches by 5 inches (12.5 x 12.5 cm). Use your spoon to put 1 ½ tablespoons (25 mL) of baking soda in the center of the square, then fold it into a square, with the baking soda inside. Make sure to tape down the folds of the time-release packet so that the baking soda stays put inside and does not fall out.

4 Into your plastic bag, POUR ½ CUP (125 ML) OF VINEGAR AND ¼ CUP (60ML) OF WARM WATER.

5 Now here's the tricky part. You need to DROP THE TIME-RELEASE PACKET INTO THE VINEGAR AND ZIP THE BAG CLOSED FAST. (When the vinegar hits the baking soda, it's going to fizz.) You can zip the bag halfway closed, then stuff the packet in and zip the bag closed the rest of the way in a hurry. Or you can put the time-release packet into the mouth of the bag and hold it up out of the vinegar by pinching the sides of the bag. Zip the bag closed and then let the packet drop into the vinegar. One way or another, get the packet in the vinegar and zip the bag closed.

6 SHAKE THE BAG a little, put it in the sink or on the ground, and stand back! The bag will puff up dramatically and pop with a bang.

7 WHY DO YOU THINK THIS HAPPENED? How is this like your body trying to fart?

YOU, ME, AND BIOLOGY

REAL-WORLD SCIENCE!

In the 1800s, a stage performer in England was known as Le Pétomane. His "act" was to fart in such a way that it sounded like music. Seriously! People paid to watch him in action. You could say that he was a "fartist"! The coolest job EVER!

SCIENCE ACTIVITY:

Test the power of fat.

FAT IS WHERE IT'S AT

WHAT DO POLAR BEARS LIKE TO EAT? Iceberg-ers!

YOU, ME, AND BIOLOGY

Polar bears spend their whole lives in places where the temperature is nearly always below freezing, and can swim in freezing water. How do they stay alive? That's easy: fat! Polar bears have a thick layer of fat beneath their skin. The fat provides (science-word alert!) **insulation**, which means the fat stops the cold from getting to the bear's insides. That's why there are no skinny polar bears! In this experiment, you'll get to see what it feels like to be a polar bear. The good news is that you do not have to hunt or eat any seals or penguins!

REAL-WORLD SCIENCE!

Three cool (not the chilly kind) facts about polar bears:

• Their fur is not white, it's transparent! The white color comes from how light reflects off the hair. Their skin is actually kinda black! A polar bear at the San Diego Zoo once turned green when algae grew in his hair!
• Hold up a ruler: That's how wide a polar bear's paw can be. Wow!
• The Inuit (Native Alaskan) name for a polar bear is Nanuk!

STUFF YOU NEED
- Vegetable shortening
- Spoon
- 2 sandwich-size zipper-lock bags
- A large container or bowl big enough for your hand
- Water
- Tray or bag of ice cubes

REAL-WORLD SCIENCE!

What do you think is the coldest place in the world? No, it's not your bathroom floor in February. The coldest temperature ever recorded was 135.8 degrees Fahrenheit below zero (−57.6 degrees Celsius), in December 2013 in Antarctica. Brrrrrr!

30

1 Take the container and fill it halfway with water. Now add several handfuls of ice cubes into the container of water so that THE CONTAINER IS FILLED ABOUT THREE-QUARTERS OF THE WAY WITH THE WATER AND ICE. Brrrr, this is going to be some really cold water.

2 Now, PUT YOUR HAND INTO THE WATER so that the water comes up to your wrist. How long can you leave your hand there? What do you feel? Okay, quick, pull your hand out. Make a note of how long you had your hand in the water. That uncomfortably cold feeling you got is what happens when the heat energy from your body is absorbed by the frigid water.

VEGETABLE SHORTENING

3 Now let's find out WHY POLAR BEARS CAN SWIM IN FREEZING WATER but humans cannot. Grab the vegetable shortening, the zipper-lock bags, and a spoon.

YOU, ME, AND BIOLOGY

4 Take one bag and FILL IT ABOUT A QUARTER FULL WITH THE SHORTENING. From the outside of the bag, press on the shortening till you get all of the air out.

5 Now, take your second zipper-lock bag and PUT YOUR HAND IN IT LIKE A MITTEN. This will protect your hand from the greasy shortening.

6 Now STICK YOUR BAG-COVERED HAND INTO THE SHORTENING BAG. Squeeze your fingers all the way to the bottom so the shortening is covering your fingers.

8 Is it different this time? WHAT DO YOU FEEL? What do you think happened this time? Now you can see just how cool fat can really be.

7 Now, PUT YOUR HAND BACK INTO THAT FREEZING TUB OF ICE WATER.

GROW YOUR OWN GERM GARDEN!

SCIENCE QUESTION:

What surface in your home has the most germs?

The skin you're in is one of the best defenses you have against a nasty enemy: germs! Germs are invisible to your eye. They're not the dust and dirt that you can see . . . they are tiny **microbes** (a science word that means "very tiny living things") that you can only see with a microscope. And they're everywhere! The germs on your skin are just waiting for you to make a mistake that lets them into your body. The inside of your body is hot, dark, and wet— just what germs need to grow. Do you want them to live in your body? No! But never fear, you already know one of the best and easiest ways to stop germs from getting in your body: wash your hands.

Where else do germs live? Let's find out. Look around your house and guess which surfaces are the most germy. Then do this experiment to find out if you were right!

STUFF YOU NEED
- Rubber gloves
- Slices of white bread
- Sandwich-size zipper-lock bags
- Water
- Tape
- Spoon

Mysophobia is the fear of germs. Soapa-phobia is the fear of washing your hands (just kidding)!

1 First, put on your rubber gloves. TAKE A SLICE OF WHITE BREAD AND RUB IT ON A SURFACE THAT YOU THINK MAY BE HIDING A LOT OF GERMS. What kinds of surfaces? Try a whole bunch—your kitchen table, the bathroom floor, the doorknob of your room, the dog's fur, your pants, your sister's hair . . . It may not look like anything is on the bread, but we'll see about that! Use a different slice for each place you want to test for germs.

2 Place each slice of bread into its own zipper-lock bag, and write the place you tested on the label. Then SPRINKLE 1 TEASPOON (5 ML) OF WATER into each bag and seal the bags shut.

3 Using tape, HANG EACH GERM BAG ON A WINDOW that gets quite a bit of sunlight. Leave the bags on the window for a week, and make daily observations. What do you think will happen?

4 All the BREAD WILL GROW MOLD. Note which bags have the fastest-growing mold or look more disgusting. (Safety tip: To prevent possible allergic reactions, do not open the bags at any time.)

5 Did you predict correctly which surface would be THE MOST GERM-RIDDEN? It looks like you proved that germs can be everywhere, even on your sister!

WHERE DO BACTERIA LIKE TO WORK OUT? At the germ-nasium!

YOU, ME, AND BIOLOGY

CHAPTER 3
AIR, AIR, EVERYWHERE

What do ants, humans, dogs, gerbils, crows, chameleons, turtles, cockroaches, and more have in common? They all breathe air! Air is actually not one thing, but a mixture of several gases. Those include oxygen, nitrogen, carbon dioxide, and hydrogen. But what's important for this chapter is not those fancy names, but one simple one: air.

What is air? Air is a gas, and gas is a state of (science word coming up) **MATTER. Matter is anything that takes up space.** The three kinds of matter are solids, liquids, and gases. Everything on earth—people, cars, books, juice, and air—is made of matter. Scientists know that air is a kind of matter that does more than provide oxygen for us to breathe. You are now going to experiment on air, and the observations you are going to make will teach you about the properties of air. Along with keeping us alive, what else can this amazing stuff do? Let's find out.

DID YOU KNOW?

Oxygen is one thing that nearly all living things cannot live without. What about fish, you say? Well, fish actually do need oxygen, and they get it from the water in a similar way to how humans get it from the air, so, yes! Fish need oxygen, too . . . they're just wetter!

What's In the Air?

The air we breathe is not just oxygen but a whole bunch of different gases. Check out this pie chart (hmmm, all of a sudden I feel hungry!) to see what's in the air.

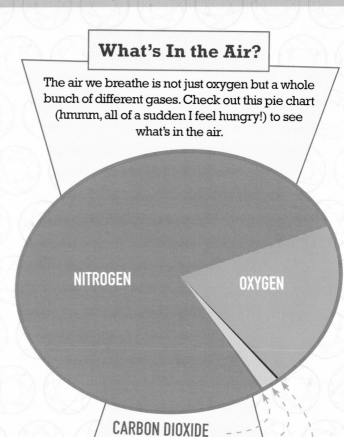

NITROGEN

OXYGEN

CARBON DIOXIDE

ARGON

ALL OTHERS Neon, Methane, Helium, Krypton, Hydrogen, Xenon, Ozone, Nitrogen Dioxide

AIR, AIR, EVERYWHERE

Look out! You're surrounded! Don't worry, though, it's not a room of invisible ninjas (though that would be cool, right?). You—and everything and everyone around you—are surrounded by air. You can't see it, but it's there, ready for you to breathe in. The "bubble" of air that surrounds Earth is more than 300 miles (485 km) thick. You breathe in about 30 pounds (13.5 kg) of air a day! Your body takes in the oxygen from the air and breathes out the carbon dioxide, which we don't need. And did you know you can thank the trees for the healthy air you breathe in? Trees take in the carbon dioxide from the air and put out oxygen. Thanks, trees!

Your first experiment is going to be to play with air and make some observations. Once you have tried each of these things—and you can come up with some of your own, too—you're going to know a lot more about what air can do!

WHAT IS THE RICHEST KIND OF AIR? A millionaire. Ha!

STUFF YOU NEED

- Balloons
- Paper
- Air pump
- Straws
- Feathers
- Pom-poms
- Tape
- Eyedropper

REAL-WORLD SCIENCE!

Have you ever seen those huge hot-air balloons floating in the sky? How do they stay up there? The answer is that hot air actually weighs less than regular air. Yes, when air is heated, it changes in a way that makes it become lighter than the cooler air around it. So it rises. When the balloons are filled with heated air, they float upward. When the pilot wants the balloon to go lower, he or she releases some of the hot air from inside the balloon to make it float back down.

REAL-WORLD SCIENCE!

You've probably heard the word **pollution**, which means the addition of unclean or harmful stuff to the environment. When we pollute, we are adding something unpleasant to the world that nature did not mean for it to have, like litter in the woods, chemicals in the water, or particles in the air. Breathing polluted air is harmful to living beings—it can make them sick. One of the main ways the air gets polluted is from smoke that comes from burning fuel that is used to power cars, factories, and buildings. Many governments pass laws to reduce the smoke. In places where there are few laws to stop pollution, the air can get so dirty that people have to wear face masks when they walk outside!

STEP by STEP

1 STICK A FEATHER INTO A STRAW AND BLOW IT OUT. What happens to the feather? Can you use the straw to keep it floating? How do you think this works?

2 BLOW UP A BALLOON AND LET IT GO. Where does it go? What happens to the air in the balloon?

3 BLOW UP A BALLOON AND LET THE AIR OUT WHILE SQUEEZING THE NOZZLE so air comes out slowly. How is it different from when you just let it go?

4 Drop different types of paper through the air and see which moves the fastest or slowest. CHANGE THE SHAPE OF THE PAPER and see what happens when different shapes are dropped through the air. How do they fall differently? Try squishing a piece of paper into a ball. What about rolling it into a worm shape?

5 Put the end of a bendy straw into a balloon and tape the balloon around the straw so no air comes out. FILL UP THE BALLOON AND LET IT GO WITH THE BENDY PART SIDEWAYS. What happens?

6 Draw air into your air pump or eyedropper. Now, take a feather and push it into the end of the air pump or eyedropper. SQUEEZE THE FEATHER HALFWAY DOWN so that the air cannot escape. Push down on the air pump or squeeze the eyedropper and watch what happens to the feather.

7 Put some pom-poms on your table and make this your target. Using your air pump, TRY AND SHOOT THE POM-POM WITH AIR. Can you hit it? How far you can get the pom-pom to go? Have an air pom-pom battle with your friends.

BUBBLE-OLOGY

What shape is a bubble? It's called a sphere (SFEER), which is a science word for "shaped like a ball."

In the last experiment, we saw that air can move solid things like feathers and balloons. But we still can't see it. Do you think it takes up space? Can something we can't see fill something up? How can we prove that? The answer is bubble-icious!

Bubbles are amazing and magical and fun—and scientific! When you make a bubble, you are trapping air inside the soapy film. Without air in there, the film would not make a bubble. When you make the bubble bigger, you prove that air has what scientists call **mass**, which is a science word for weight. Let's get a little soapy and see how we can prove that air takes up space!

BUBBLE RECORDS

(Yes, there are some! I know! I was surprised, too!)

In 2005, John Erck blew a bubble big enough to hold 13,000 baseballs!

In 1999, Fan Yang made a wall out of bubbles. The wall was 156 feet (47 m) long and 13 feet (4 m) high!

In 1999, at an English soccer game, 23,680 people blew bubbles at the same time. Yes, it made it into the *Guinness Book of World Records!*

STUFF YOU NEED
- 8-ounce (240 mL) or larger spray bottle
- 1 ounce (30 mL) glycerin (you can pick this up at a pharmacy)
- 3 ounces (90 mL) dishwashing soap
- 1 cup (240 mL) water
- 1 sheet US letter-size cardstock

GLYCERIN

1 To make great bubbles, TAKE A CUP OF WATER AND ADD 3 OUNCES (90 ML) OF DISHWASHING SOAP (product placement alert: I find that the Joy brand works best!)

2 Next, ADD THE SECRET INGREDIENT, 1 ounce (30 mL) of glycerin. Stir gently. (bubble expert tip: The glycerin slows down the rate at which the water will evaporate and is the secret to longer-lasting bubbles.)

3 The hardest step: COVER THE BUBBLE SOLUTION AND LEAVE IT OVERNIGHT. This allows chemicals that might interfere with the bubbles to evaporate. Honestly, have patience, and you'll have better bubbles! (Patience is not really a science word, but it's a quality all good scientists need!)

4 After a day, you and your bubble solution can have some fun! Roll the cardstock into a cone. Cut the tip off the large end so the bottom of the cone is flat. Dip the large end into the cup . . . and then blow into the small end. CONGRATULATIONS . . . IT'S A BUBBLE!

5 Now it's time to EXPERIMENT AND INVESTIGATE: What happens if you blow a bubble onto your hand? What if your hand is wet? Can you blow a bubble onto a table? How about a wet table? Note what happens.

National Bubble Week is the third week of March. Get bubbly!

6 Let's get big! PUT A LOT OF AIR IN THE BUBBLE. Does the bubble get bigger? Smaller? How much can you put in? What does this tell you about whether air takes up space?

AIR, AIR, EVERYWHERE

SCIENCE
ACTIVITY:

Prove that air
takes up space.

THE MAGIC OF AIR

WHAT DO YOU
GET WHEN YOU
GRADUATE FROM
DIVING SCHOOL?
A deep-loma.

Time to put on your top hat and get out your magic wand. (I personally prefer a Prestidigito 3XZ-1000, but you might have your own favorites. I call mine "Wandy.") We're going to use science to perform a magic trick. No, I have not made a machine that will make your bed (though, of course, since you're an inventor now, I bet YOU could make one of those!). This trick will stun and amaze your friends, and only you will know the scientific secret behind it all.

The science behind this trick is the science of **matter**. Everything in the universe is made up of matter, and matter takes up space. The three basic kinds of matter are **solids**, **liquids**, and **gases**. Air is a gas. And yes, gas takes up space. It's in front of your face. It's on top of your hair. It's even under your underwear. If you don't believe me, try this experiment.

STUFF YOU NEED
- Cup
- Paper towel
- Tape
- Container of water larger than the cup

REAL-WORLD SCIENCE!

In the 16th century, scientists used the ideas behind this experiment to invent diving bells. By lowering the huge iron bells underwater just right, they could sit high and dry inside and look out at the fish below!

STEP by STEP

 1 **LOOK INTO THE EMPTY CUP. What is inside?** Nothing, right? (Okay, yes, smartypants . . . there is air in there, but we're not talking about that!)

2 **TAKE A PAPER TOWEL** and crush it as hard as you can into the shape of a ball. Now take a piece of tape and roll it up so that it is sticky on all of its sides. Stick this tape roll to the bottom of the paper towel ball.

3 Take the balled-up paper towel and **PUSH IT ALL THE WAY TO THE BOTTOM OF THE CUP.** Make sure that you squeeze it as far down as you can get it.

 4 **FILL THE LARGER CONTAINER ABOUT THREE-QUARTERS FULL OF WATER.** Then, take your cup with the towel in it and turn it upside down.

5 Take the cup that is now upside down and **PUT IT DIRECTLY INTO THE CONTAINER OF WATER.** Don't let it go in sideways. Make sure that it is completely submerged under the water. Leave it there for 10 seconds.

6 **What happened? WHY DID THE TOWEL REMAIN DRY?** Was the cup really empty when you put it into the water?

BONUS INVENTION STORY

Remember how some things are invented by accident? Here's another one. Arthur Scott owned a paper company. In 1907, his company made a whole railroad car full of toilet paper that was too thick. He didn't want to throw it away, so he made the sheets bigger and sold them as single-use paper towels for wiping the nose instead of tissue for wiping the butt!

AIR, AIR, EVERYWHERE

41

Does air have strength?

THE POWER OF AIR

The wheels on the bus go round and round, right? But they won't go anywhere without air! When you're riding on a bus or in a car, you're not riding just on rubber tires. Those tires are filled with air. That shows just how strong and useful air can be. Can you imagine riding on wooden tires (the first bicycles had wooden wheels). That would make for a pretty uncomfortable ride!

Air can be one of the most powerful forces around. When it's wind, it can be strong enough to knock over trees or buildings. When rushing under wings, it can make an airplane stay in the air. When blown through a straw, it can make bubbles that annoy your big sister! (Okay, that's not really that strong . . . but it is funny!) When air is **compressed** (a science word that means "squeezed") into a tight space—for example, the air in a tire—it can lift up a whole school bus. Let's do an experiment to prove that air has strength.

REAL-WORLD SCIENCE!

How do you measure air? Scientists—and you—use an air pressure gauge. It measures how much pressure per square inch (PSI) the air is putting on an object. Look at your bike or car tires: Find the numbers on them. They tell you what the right PSI is for that tire!

WHAT IS LIGHTER THAN A FEATHER BUT EVEN THE STRONGEST PERSON IN THE WORLD CAN'T LIFT IT? Air!

1 In the zipper-lock bag, **MAKE A SMALL HOLE.**

2 **SLIP A STRAW INTO THE HOLE** to about halfway down the straw's length. Use tape to seal up the hole around the straw.

3 Make sure to **LEAVE ABOUT HALF OF THE STRAW IN THE BAG AND THE OTHER END STICKING OUT** of the bag.

4 Now, **PUT A SMALL BOOK ON THE BAG.**

5 5. Using the straw, **BLOW UP THE BAG:** What happens to the book?

Typhoons and hurricanes can have winds that are more than 240 miles (385 km) per hour . . . that's faster than a NASCAR race car.

6 Keep trying more books to see how strong air can be (or how strong your lungs can make it!). **HOW MANY CAN YOU RAISE UP USING THE POWER OF AIR?**

Engineers can raise enormous sunken ships with air. They put huge bags under the ships, then fill the bags with air. And up come the ships from the depths!

AIR, AIR, EVERYWHERE

43

FLYING WATER

WHAT DID THE SINK SAY TO THE WATER FAUCET? You're a real drip.

We have spent a lot of time experimenting with air and learning about its amazing properties. Perhaps the coolest property of air is what happens when it moves really fast. You know what is even cooler? What happens to things when air moves really fast around them!

Think of an airplane: When it rolls down the runway, the fast-moving air whooshing under its wings makes this giant solid plane lift into the air.

The reasons can be found in **Bernoulli's principle**, which tells us that the faster the air is moving, the less pressure it is exerting. Do you know what happens then? I do: Liftoff!

Now, wait a second—we know that solid things airplanes can take off, but how about liquids? Can we make water fly? Let's test it and see.

AIR, AIR, EVERYWHERE

WHAT'S THE DIFFERENCE BETWEEN A FLY AND A BIRD? A bird can fly, but a fly can't bird!

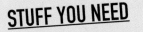
STUFF YOU NEED

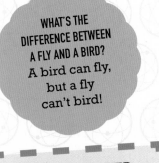
- Cup
- Water
- 2 straws
- A lot of strong moving air

WRIGHT ON!

You know that the **Wright brothers** invented the airplane . . . um, right? Well, they did, way back in 1903. They also invented the wind tunnel. They created a machine that blew air really fast over samples of their wing designs. (They didn't use a straw like you did, though.) They watched what the air did and adjusted their designs to make them work better!

THANKS, DAN!

Daniel Bernoulli was a Swiss scientist who lived in the 1700s. He studied liquids and how they moved. He used math to describe these movements. He's the guy who came up with the ideas that eventually led to powered flight!

1 Get a cup and **FILL IT UP WITH WATER.** Now place one of the straws in the water.

2 Cut the second straw in half; this will be your blower. Now take this blower and hold it perpendicular (at a right angle, see the picture below) to the straw that is in the water. **PREPARE TO TAKE A DEEP BREATH AND BLOW AS HARD AS YOU CAN THROUGH THE STRAW.** What do you think is going to happen when you blow across the top of the straw in the water with your other straw (blower)?

TIME OUT! Remember! Science is all about making predictions, so please make a prediction before testing it. **TIME IN!**

3 Okay, **BLOW ACROSS THE TOP OF THE STRAW THAT IS IN THE WATER** really hard with your blower.

4 What happened? Did the water fly up through the straw? Did it blow clear across the table? **YOU MADE THE WATER HAVE LIFT** (which, in science, means a force that moves something upward).

5 **THINK ABOUT IT:** The fast-moving air that was blowing across the top of the straw in the cup reduced the air pressure and the water flew into the air.

6 **TRY THIS EXPERIMENT AGAIN** using a different-sized straw as the blower and see what happens.

AIR, AIR, EVERYWHERE

HELICOPT-
AIR!

STUFF YOU NEED:
- Paper
- Ruler
- Scissors
- Paper clips
- Stopwatch

I don't know about you, but I love making things that can fly into the air. Can you think of a few machines that fly? Of all flying machines, my personal favorite is the helicopter. I'll tell you why: A helicopter can lift from a resting position straight up into the air. Planes cannot do this. I know what you are thinking—how can we make a helicopter at home? Believe it or not, you can!

You're going to be a flight engineer and make a paper helicopter that will give us the opportunity to test important principles of flight, including some of the things you learned in the previous experiment:

• When we rapidly push air out of the way of our flying machine, it lowers the air pressure around it.

• When there is an area of higher air pressure underneath an area of low pressure, it gives the flying object **lift**.

Science is all about asking questions! This cool little poem will help you remember:

Investigation
In the science nation:
Make an observation.
What a cool sensation!

REAL-WORLD
SCIENCE!

Helicopter shapes are also found in nature. Lots of seeds have "wings" that help them float to new areas where they can sprout. One example is the sycamore tree seed.

WRIGHT **ON!**
PART II

The **Wright brothers** were inspired to learn more about flying when they were kids thanks to a toy propeller. Their dad brought them a gadget that flew into the air when it was wound up. The Wrights thought this was awesome and remembered it when they started to build their airplane.

1 CUT A RECTANGLE that is about 3 inches by 5 inches (7.5 x 12 cm) out of paper. You can make it bigger if you want to.

2 CUT DOWN THE CENTER of the paper to almost half way, splitting the top into two flaps.

3 FOLD DOWN ONE OF THE FLAPS. Turn the paper over, and fold down the other flap in the opposite direction.

4 Lift up the flaps so that they are at a 90-degree angle (like an L). Now THEY FORM YOUR PROPELLER.

5 About a quarter-inch (1 cm) below the propeller, CUT A SLIT ABOUT ONE-THIRD THE WIDTH OF THE PAPER. When this is done, please do this again on the other side.

6 Now FOLD IN ONE SIDE OF THE BASE AND THEN THE OTHER so that your paper helicopter is the shape of a letter T.

7 USE A PAPER CLIP TO HOLD THE FOLDS TOGETHER at the bottom of the helicopter.

8 Okay, now we can TOSS THE HELICOPTER INTO THE AIR or drop it from somewhere high. What happens? Throw it really fast into the air and observe what happens.

9 TURN YOUR HELICOPTER UPSIDE DOWN AND DROP IT. What happens? Can you get your paper helicopter to spin the other way?

AIR, AIR, EVERYWHERE

47

STRAW ROCKET

SCIENCE QUESTION:

What is an aerodynamic shape?

AIR, AIR, EVERYWHERE

Wow! This air stuff is really amazing. We have seen that air can move things. We proved that air takes up space by making giant bubbles. We even used moving air to make water fly!

However, we have yet to make something solid fly through the air. This is what we are about to do!

When something moves through the air quickly—like a jet, a curveball, or a model rocket—we say it is aerodynamic.

Your goal is to construct something that will move quickly through the air. The best part is that you can make changes to your final product to see if you can get it to go farther. Science is a process, so you may have to redesign your straw rocket several times until you get your desired results. It took the Wright brothers three years to build their perfect airplane . . . let's hope you don't need that long!

STUFF YOU NEED
- Paper
- Pencil
- Tape
- Drinking straw

ROCKET FACTS

- To escape Earth's gravity, rockets have to travel about 25,000 miles per hour (40,250 kph).
- Chinese warriors in the 1200s used mini-rockets made of bamboo to fire missiles at their enemies.
- In the "Star-Spangled Banner," the words "rockets' red glare" came from the weapons the British were firing at the American Fort McHenry in 1812. Francis Scott Key, who wrote the song, watched those rockets fly!

STEP by STEP

HOW DID THE ROCKET LOSE ITS JOB? It got fired!

1 CUT OUT A 6-INCH BY 6-INCH (15 X 15 CM) PIECE OF PAPER. Use regular printing paper so that it is not too heavy.

2 WRAP THIS SQUARE OF PAPER AROUND A PENCIL. When you wrap it around the pencil, make sure it is wrapped very tightly. You should now have a really tight cylinder (a tube-shape.) Tape down the sides of the paper.

3 Pull the pencil out of the cylinder. Now YOU HAVE THE BODY OF YOUR ROCKET.

4 Fold down a bit of the top of the cylinder and tape it. This way YOU HAVE AN OPEN END AND A CLOSED END to your rocket.

5 You can CREATE WINGS WITH EXTRA PAPER for the open end of your rocket. You can make these wings any shape you like. (Idea time: Use differently shaped wings to see how your rocket flies with each kind.)

6 When you're READY TO LAUNCH, put your paper rocket onto one end of your straw—and blow into the other end!

7 WHAT HAPPENS WHEN YOU BLOW HARD? OR SOFTLY? What happens when you change the angle of the rocket? Did your rocket go far? How can we make it go farther? What changes can you make that get it to go faster? How can you make it more aerodynamic? What if you made a cone-shaped top on the rocket?

THE FATHER OF ROCKETRY

American scientist **Robert Goddard** invented modern rockets. He was the first to make a rocket that used liquid fuel to achieve great heights. His ideas led directly to the rocket ships that later blasted humans and satellites into space.

AIR, AIR, EVERYWHERE

CHAPTER 4

DON'T FEAR . . . BE AN ENGINEER!

See that building? An engineer helped make it. Did you ride in a car or a train today? An engineer helped design and build it. That street outside, the refrigerator in your house, the TV you watch, the computer you work on: All of them were created (at least partly) by engineers. Engineers use science and technology to create objects of just about every size imaginable. In this section, we're going to focus mostly on engineers who design and build bridges, tunnels, skyscrapers, and vehicles. They have to use a lot of science to make sure the structures they build don't fall down! They learn chemistry so that they know how building materials go together. They learn physics so they can balance their structures. They even have to study the weather to see what that wind and water could do to the things they build. In this chapter, YOU are the engineer.

HARD AT WORK

Engineers do many different jobs.
Here are just a few types of engineers and what they do.

STRUCTURAL ENGINEERS: design and build buildings and bridges

MECHANICAL ENGINEERS: build machines like mighty motors

ELECTRICAL ENGINEERS: design systems that bring power to buildings and cities

COMPUTER ENGINEERS: make computer systems

DON'T FEAR . . . BE AN ENGINEER!

IN THIS CHAPTER:

THE WORLD'S STRONGEST CARDBOARD

Buildings come in all shapes and sizes, but somehow they all stay up (except sometimes in a big earthquake, but we'll deal with that in Chapter Five). However, you might notice that some shapes are used again and again in many buildings, and that's because these shapes create structures that are strong and durable. One of the most important is the **column** (say *KOLL-um*; the "n" is silent). A column is a cylinder, which is the shape of a straw or a tube (remember?). Engineers know that columns can work alone or together to hold up a lot of weight. Columns are often used to hold up heavy loads, such as the roofs of buildings. The heavy load pushes on the column (this is called **compression**,) but it is strong enough to stay up. By building columns in the right places, engineers can make even very large buildings very safe. For our first engineering activity, we're going to test the strength of a column.

REAL-WORLD SCIENCE!

The ancient Greeks and Romans, who built many large structures—some of which are still standing today, thousands of years after they were erected—knew how important columns are.

Most large buildings today are made of concrete poured over a frame. The steel is in the form of rods or bars. The steel pieces are called **reinforcing bars** . . . or (science-word alert) rebar for short. Look around your school or your house and see if you can find columns that are holding up the walls and ceiling. They might be squares instead of circular.

STUFF YOU NEED

- Sheet of cardstock, about the size of a regular piece of paper
- Tape
- Stack of books

WHAT DID ONE WALL SAY TO THE OTHER WALL? I'll meet you at the corner.

1 ROLL ONE SHEET OF CARDSTOCK OR VERY THIN CARDBOARD INTO A CYLINDER SHAPE. Tap it on a flat surface so the top edges are even. Now tape along the sides so that the column/cylinder keeps its shape. (Secret backup plan: If you can't find cardstock, you can use an empty paper towel roll . . . but it might not be as much fun.)

2 CHECK THAT YOUR COLUMN IS STRAIGHT and even so that it can stand up and remain balanced.

4 Start adding books one by one onto your column— S-L-O-W-L-Y—so that it does not lose its balance. KEEP ADDING BOOKS until the column eventually collapses.

3 Do you think this column can hold a book? More than one? Before you try, predict how many you think your column can hold. Then IT'S TIME TO TEST! Carefully place a book on top of your column—is it holding? Remember, science is all about asking questions, making predictions, testing them, and getting results.

WHAT DID THE GROUND SAY TO THE EARTHQUAKE? You crack me up!

5 How many books did your column hold? Was your prediction correct? WHY DO YOU THINK WHAT HAPPENED . . . happened?! Can you figure out why?

DON'T FEAR . . . BE AN ENGINEER!

THE WORLD'S STRONGEST BALLOONS

CARMELO SAYS:

This activity will be mu[ch] more fun with a grou[p] of friends. Or a group [of] enemies. Just as long a[s] they are people and n[ot] cats or dogs.

Have you ever popped a balloon? It's pretty surprising . . . and loud! They pop for many reasons, but sometimes it's because they got squashed. Did you know that balloons can actually be very strong? Let's find out how and why that might be true. In this activity, we're going to make a column of air (remember what columns are?) . . . and stand on it! But this column won't be standing straight up and down like a paper towel roll . . . this column will be horizontal, a direction word that means side-to-side, like the floor. The opposite is vertical, or up-and-down, like a wall.

First, a bit of balloon-popping fun. Fill up a balloon and tie it tight. Then sit on it! What do you think will happen? Then try standing on it. What happens?

You probably popped all the balloons with your mighty weight. But we're going to prove that there is strength in numbers . . . or at least in columns.

STUFF YOU NEED
- Tape
- Balloons
- Piece of cardboard about 2 feet by 2 feet (60 cm x 60 cm)
- Markers

WHAT TYPE OF MUSIC ARE BALLOONS AFRAID OF?
Pop music!

STEP *by* **STEP**

WHAT DOES
A BABY BALLOON
NEVER CALL ITS
FATHER?
Pop!

1 Fill up three good-sized balloons and tape them down to a piece of cardboard that is so that the balloons are side by side. Now tape three more balloons down so that you have two rows of three balloons. Remember to TAPE THE BALLOONS DOWN. The easiest way to do this is to roll a piece of tape so that it is sticky on all sides, then stick the piece of tape to the balloon and press it firmly down onto the cardboard. Note: The cardboard should be a little bigger than your rows of balloons.

2 When you have completed the platform, lay it on the ground so that the balloons are touching the floor and the cardboard is sitting on top. The SIX BALLOONS FORM A COLUMN OF AIR below the platform.

3 Now the fun part: GENTLY STAND ON YOUR AIR-COLUMN PLATFORM. It is a good idea to have some helpers around you as you balance on the platform. Don't jump on it.

4 What happened? DID THE BALLOONS POP? What happens if you stand on it and have one of your helpers pop one of the balloons? Are you still standing? How many balloons do you need to have filled to keep the platform from collapsing?

5 Discuss how we have proved that A COLUMN SHAPE IS VERY STRONG FOR BUILDING.

DON'T FEAR . . . BE AN ENGINEER!

THE LEANING TOWER OF STRAWS-A

How high can you build?

STUFF YOU NEED
- Box of long drinking straws
- Moldable clay

STRAWS

Who needs to buy plastic bricks to build with? We can build a tower with just straws and clay. How high can you make yours? The science part is picking the right shape.

This experiment will test your engineering ability. Try out different shapes for your building and see which ones can be taller and which are more stable. Do you need a bigger base? Do you need more columns? Do different shapes make for a more stable building? Remember the columns you built earlier . . . can that shape help you build a skyscraper?

We're going to use only straws (as the columns) and clay (as the connectors). There is no right answer to this experiment. It is a chance for you to try out new ideas and see which work the best. That's what science is all about!

REAL-WORLD SCIENCE!

In Pisa, Italy, the famous Leaning Tower is just that—a tall tower that is leaning over quite a bit. Construction of the tower began in 1173 but took 200 years! During that time, an edge of the tower's bottom started to sink into the ground. The tower soon started to lean to one side, but it didn't fall over. You can climb it today and feel what it's like to be in an unbalanced building! In 2008, engineers went to work on the tower. They didn't straighten it out, but they did reinforce it . . . so now it won't lean any more than it already does!

1 Start by forming small balls of clay, each about the size of a dime. **THIS WILL BE LIKE THE MORTAR** (a substance that fills up the spaces between building materials like bricks or stones—or, in this case, straws—and holds them together) between your straw columns. Believe it or not, the ancient Egyptians used a mortar that is actually stronger that the rock that they used to build the pyramids. This is why they are still standing after thousands of years! It really bonded the stones together.

BULDING TIPS

Could a structure with three sides be stronger than one with four sides? What do you think? Could triangles be stronger than squares? Why? Straws arranged into triangles form more stable shapes than straws that are arranged into squares. When force (weight) is applied to the joints, a triangle changes shape less than a square. (You wouldn't want a bridge or a building to change shape when weight was put on it, right?) When force is applied to a square, as shown below, the joints (the places where the sides meet) move, and the shape changes. In a triangle, the cross-piece at the bottom helps to hold the side together, so they do not move. Three sides are in this case stronger than four.

2 **PUT THE CLAY BALLS AT THE ENDS OF EACH STRAW.** Look at different geometric shapes you can make with the straws.

3 Start putting the shapes together to make a structure. **YOU'RE IN CHARGE,** so it can be any shape you want. Each straw counts as one story or one floor. How many floors high you can make your structure?

5 Eventually, **GRAVITY WILL WIN.** But what could you change to make your building higher?

4 If your structure collapses, **TRY AGAIN.**

DON'T FEAR . . . BE AN ENGINEER!

BUILDING BIG

Here are five of the tallest buildings in the world:

Burj Khalifa, Dubai	830 meters	2,723 feet
Makkah Royal Clock Tower Hotel	601 meters	1,971 feet
Taipei 101	508 meters	1,666 feet
Shanghai World Financial Center	482 meters	1,581 feet

The tallest building in the United States is **One World Trade Center** in New York City. It's 1,776 feet (541 m) high.

PAPER BRIDGE

We have already seen how a piece of cardstock paper can be made to support the weight of a lot of books. We never assumed that a piece of paper can hold all of this weight, which is why the science of architecture is simply amazing! Let's look at another major piece of marvelous architecture: a bridge.

Bridges stretch across waterways or canyons or highways so people and vehicles can cross over. They have to be designed very carefully. You wouldn't want to be on a bridge in your car if the bridge fell down! Engineers use a lot of science to make sure their bridge designs are strong and safe. Over the centuries, they have tried many different shapes so that they know which shapes work best for each bridge. In this activity, you're going to be a bridge engineer. You'll experiment with different shapes to see which work best. Make sure to predict what you think will happen and record what really does happen.

I'm glad engineers create models like the ones you will make. That makes me feel much safer when I drive across a bridge!

REAL-WORLD SCIENCE!

The world's highest bridge is the Sidu River Bridge in China. Don't look down when you cross . . . it's more than 1,600 feet (480 m) above the canyon below! The longest bridge in the United States is more than 24 miles (38 km) long! The Lake Pontchartrain Causeway connects two cities in the state of Louisiana. A bridge in Turkey was built more than 2,800 years ago . . . and it's still used today! It's considered the world's oldest working bridge.

STUFF YOU NEED
- Paper
- Pennies
- Stack of books
- Paper clips
- Pencil and notebook to record results
- Creativity!

NOTES

The most common types of bridges are beam, truss, cantilever, arch, tied arch, suspension, and cable-stayed.

1 Place a sheet of paper flat across two books that are placed about 10 inches (25 cm) apart. THAT'S YOUR BRIDGE! How many pennies do you think the bridge will hold?

2 Once your predictions are done, TEST YOUR FLAT-PAPER BRIDGE. Add pennies one at a time so that when the bridge collapses you will know exactly how many pennies it held. Place the pennies near the middle of your bridge. How many pennies did the bridge hold? Three? Five? More?

3 From your observations, you can see that a flat sheet of paper cannot hold many pennies. WHAT DO YOU THINK YOU CAN DO TO THE PAPER TO MAKE IT HOLD MORE PENNIES? Do you remember the column experiment? Changing the shape of your support can make a big difference!

4 WHAT CAN YOU DO TO MAKE THE PAPER STRONGER? Remember, every time you make a redesign, you should also make a prediction, test it, and record your results. Try to construct a bridge that can hold the most pennies.

5 What if you rolled up the paper? Test it and see how many pennies that would hold. What about an accordion shape? Try other types of folds. Try placing the pennies in different places on your bridge. Try using your paper clips to help support and stiffen the paper. THERE ARE MANY, MANY BRIDGE DESIGNS THAT YOU CAN CREATE, SO GET CREATIVE.

6 WHAT DESIGN WAS THE STRONGEST? How do you think changing the shape of the paper helped your bridge resist the bending forces created by the pennies?

DON'T FEAR . . . BE AN ENGINEER!

Build a car out of ordinary household materials.

LEAN, MEAN DRIVING MACHINE

Do you know that people have been using simple machines for thousands of years? Simple machines make physical work easier by allowing us to push and pull more weight over more distance than we could on our own. The ancient Egyptians used simple machines to carry stones that weighed thousands of pounds across the sandy desert to build the pyramids. Back in the days of the Renaissance (from the 14th to the 17th century) scientists defined six devices as simple machines. You have probably seen or used most of them! The inclined plane is basically a flat surface tilted on an angle, like a ramp; the lever is a long bar that you push against a supporting point; the pulley uses a wheel and rope to raise and lower something heavy; the wedge has a slanted side and a sharp edge for cutting; the screw helps things hold together; and then, there's my favorite— the wheel and axle. The wheel and axle (basically, a wheel with a rod through the middle) has been used for more than 5,000 years. Do you know of any machines that we use today that have a wheel and axle? Right! Bicycles, wagons, cars, buses, and motorcycles all use a wheel and axle.

Wouldn't it be cool if you could engineer your own machine using a wheel and axle? Well, why don't you? I bet you have everything you need lying around your house, so why don't we get started?

STUFF YOU NEED

- Straws
- Life Savers candy
- Cardstock or cardboard at least 5 inches (10 cm) square
- Paper clips
- Tape
- Pictures of cars

1 CUT OUT A 5-INCH (10-CM) SQUARE from cardstock or a piece of cardboard.

2 Now take your straws and tape one straw across the top of your square so the ends of the straw stick out on each side. Make sure that you tape it down securely. Repeat this process and tape the other straw on the same side at the bottom of the square. THESE ARE GOING TO BE YOUR AXLES.

3 TAKE ONE LIFE SAVERS CANDY AND SLIDE IT ONTO THE STRAW until it hits the paper. Tape around the end of the straw so that the end of the straw becomes bigger. This will stop the wheel from falling off like the nut-and-bolt that holds a car wheel in place. Repeat this process at each corner of each straw.

4 When this is done, place the car down so that the wheels are on the floor. GIVE YOUR CAR A PUSH (force) and observe its movements across the floor.

5 What happens when you blow on your car? DOES IT MOVE? Try pushing your car with a strong force and observe what happens.

6 TRY BRINGING ANOTHER SIMPLE MACHINE LIKE AN INCLINED PLANE INTO THE EXPERIMENT. (Remember, an inclined plane is a flat surface on an angle.) Set up a flat piece of cardstock like a hill, and observe what happens when your car is released from the top of the inclined plane.

7 CAN YOU SEE HOW SIMPLE MACHINES MAKE WORK EASIER? Can you make changes to your car that will make it move faster?

REAL-WORLD SCIENCE!

Some cool facts about cars:
• The first car to be powered by a gas engine was made in 1886 by Karl Benz in Germany.
• The Ford Model T was the first car to be made in huge quantities on an assembly line. It was first sold in 1908.
• The bestselling car of all time is the Toyota Corolla. More than 40 million have been sold since it was first made in 1974.

DON'T FEAR . . . BE AN ENGINEER!

HOVERCRAFT AHOY!

WHAT GOES IN CARS BUT COMES OUT OF PEOPLE? Gas!

DON'T FEAR ... BE AN ENGINEER!

Okay, you really are an engineer! Since starting this book, you have constructed buildings, bridges, and cars—now it's time for a flying machine! Do you think a machine can zip across your floor ... without wheels? Yes! It's called a hovercraft, a machine that rides on a cushion of air.

A hovercraft usually works best on water. By rising up to just skim over the waves, the craft needs less energy to fight the friction of the water. A hovercraft moving on land has no friction at all; it rises off the ground before moving forward.

Start this activity with a little artwork. Get your markers and draw on the top of the CD (compact disc) so it looks really cool. IMPORTANT: Write and draw on the side that is not mirrored. Come up with a fun name for your hovercraft, too!

The mini-marshmallows on your materials list will be your crash test dummy ... er, passenger! Feel free to decorate him or her as well!

Also, for part of this you will need help from an adult. So tell your adult to come in and sit down and wait for instructions. After all, you're the scientist here!

STUFF YOU NEED
- Old CD (compact disc; make sure it is one that you don't use anymore!)
- Mini-marshmallows
- Balloons
- Cap from a water bottle that pushes up and down to open and close
- Permanent markers
- Hot-glue gun
- Pennies

1. Ask your adult helper to use a hot-glue gun to **ATTACH A WATER-BOTTLE TOP (OPEN SIDE UP) TO THE CENTER OF YOUR CD.** Remember, your bottle cap should pull up to open and push down to close. Make sure that the opening hole and the hole in the CD are not covered with any glue.

2. Once the glue is dry, it's time to **TEST YOUR HOVERCRAFT.** Inflate a balloon and squeeze the neck of the balloon so that the air does not escape. Place the inflated balloon over the closed bottle top. This will prevent the air from escaping. When you are ready, place the hovercraft on a smooth surface.

3. **PULL UP ON THE BOTTLE TOP,** and the air from the balloon will begin to escape, causing your hovercraft to move across the surface.

4. **TEST YOUR HOVERCRAFT ON DIFFERENT SURFACES.** What happens if you try it on a rug? How about a smooth wooden floor? On what surface did your hovercraft move the farthest?

5. If you **GIVE IT A GENTLE PUSH** while the air is escaping, does it go farther?

6. What happens if you add weight to the hovercraft? Try adding pennies and see what happens. Remember **THE BEAUTY OF ENGINEERING IS HAVING THE ABILITY TO CREATE REDESIGNS.** Have fun and explore with your new flying machine!

REAL-WORLD SCIENCE!

Hovercraft (also known as air-cushioned vehicles or ACVs) are in use on waterways around the world, as passenger or car ferries, as rescue vehicles, and for military uses. For several decades, a hovercraft carried people and cars across the English Channel. When a tunnel opened under that waterway, the hovercraft stopped running. Hovercraft are still used for short trips across northern European waterways and in Hong Kong. You can ride small hovercraft on some lakes in the United States, such as in Florida and Idaho.

DON'T FEAR . . . BE AN ENGINEER!

What makes a rocket zoom through space?

BALLOON ROCKET

To escape gravity, a rocket ha[s] to travel at more than 250,000 miles (400,000 km) per hour!

When I was a kid, I always dreamed of rockets. I still love them! They can move so fast and they can travel so far. I love how they just seem to defy the laws of gravity. I love that they took astronauts into space and carried satellites high above the Earth. In fact, I love them so much, I'm going to show you how to make one right now!

And to make it, we'll just use more of that stuff that's lying around in your junk drawer, waiting to be blasted into orbit.

So how do rockets work? Everything on Earth moves because of a force. We are going to use air as our force and make our rocket zoom across your home.

STUFF YOU NEED
- String measuring 10 feet (3 m)
- Round balloons
- Chairs
- Tape
- Straws

ROCKET FACTS

- The tallest rocket ever launched was the Saturn V. It was flown by NASA in the 1960s and stood more than 300 feet (100 m) tall. It could carry 120 tons (110 t) into space. A Russian rocket called the Proton has been announced; if built, it will carry 160 tons (150 t)!
- Each of the fuel tanks for the space shuttle held 1 million gallons (3.8 million L) of rocket fuel! All of it burned up in just about two minutes.
- Model rockets built and launched by kids have flown thousands of feet in the air; why don't you ask an adult to check out model rockets with you? You can find models to make at local hobby shops.

STEP by STEP

1 TIE ONE END OF THE STRING TO ONE END OF A CHAIR.

2 PUT THE STRING THROUGH THE STRAW, like you are threading a needle.

3 Pull the string tight and carry the other end across the room to another end of a chair. TIE IT TO THE SECOND CHAIR.

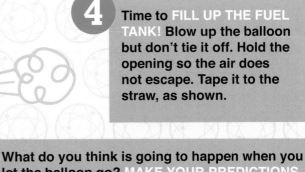

4 Time to FILL UP THE FUEL TANK! Blow up the balloon but don't tie it off. Hold the opening so the air does not escape. Tape it to the straw, as shown.

5 What do you think is going to happen when you let the balloon go? MAKE YOUR PREDICTIONS and test them by letting go of the balloon.

6 What happened? DID YOU NOTICE THE DIRECTION THAT THE AIR CAME OUT OF THE BALLOON? The air came out one way, and yet the balloon went the opposite direction. As air came out of the balloon, it created a forward motion called thrust. Real rockets use the same principle. The rocket burns rocket fuel, which pushes downward, and the rocket takes off. We have liftoff!!!

7 Have fun with your balloon rocket and try different things. What happens if you USE DIFFERENT-SIZED BALLOONS? Does it go faster? Farther?

8 HOW FAR CAN YOU GET YOUR BALLOON ROCKET TO TRAVEL? Ask different questions and have fun testing them all to get your amazing results.

DON'T FEAR . . . BE AN ENGINEER!

CHAPTER 5

NATURAL DISASTERS

Earth does not stand still. We know we're spinning around and around in space . . . and we know we're whizzing around the sun, too. But back here on Earth, the land and the sea and even the air move around a lot, too. Usually, that's a good thing. But sometimes, the earth, sea, or air can do things that aren't so good for living beings. An earthquake makes the ground shake and shift beneath our feet, knocking over buildings and collapsing bridges. A volcano can spit out vast clouds of black smoke and blazing hot lava streams. Tornadoes can swoop down, destroying houses and even whole neighborhoods. Rivers can rise till they overflow and flood, while mud can cause a whole hillside to slide downward. These are all called **natural disasters**. In this chapter, we'll learn much more about what causes them . . . and you'll get a chance to cause some (small ones) of your own!

We'll look at what is inside the earth (that's the science of geology). We'll see how an earthquake makes buildings fall (that's physics!). And we'll watch a tornado in action (that's meteorology). Get out your hard hat and let's get to work!

REAL-WORLD SCIENCE!

We can actually measure the force of an earthquake, using something called the **Richter** (RICK-ter) scale. It was invented by American scientist named Charles Richter in 1935. A measurement of 2 or 3 is a small earthquake that just shakes things up a bit—sometimes people can sleep right through a small earthquake. A measurement of 6 or 7 is a really bad jolt that can knock over buildings! The highest number ever recorded was 9.5 for a 1960 quake in Chile.

NATURAL DISASTER?

There are many forces at work in nature, and sometimes they can cause dangerous situations. Here is a chart of some natural disasters. I might have put some other, human disasters in there, too. See if you can spot them!

AVALANCHE a massive snowslide
EARTHQUAKE a vibration of the ground
VOLCANIC ERUPTION a volcano shooting out steam and lava
BARF ERUPTION your little brother throws up
FLOOD a body of water overflows
TSUNAMI a gigantic water wave
FARTSTORM a blast of stinky air from your butt
HURRICANE a huge tropical storm
BURP BURST puffs of stinky air from your stomach come out of your mouth
TORNADO a spinning column of air
DIAPER EXPLOSION your baby sister
WILDFIRE an uncontrolled forest fire

IN THIS CHAPTER:

LAYERS OF THE EARTH

WHAT SHAKES
AND IS EDIBLE?
An
earthcake!

Look up and you can see what's in the sky. Clouds, the sun and moon, stars at night. Look down, however, and though you can see the surface, you can't really see what's inside the Earth. Do you ever wonder what our planet is made of? If you took the universe's biggest samurai sword and sliced the Earth in half, what would you see? Well, of course, you'd see a heck of a lot of angry people! But just pretend.

What you'd see is that the inside of the earth is made in layers, like lasagna or birthday cake. Do you want to find out what those layers look like—and to learn something really amazing about Earth?

In this experiment, you're going to build a replica of planet Earth . . . from scratch! Actually, from clay, but "scratch" sounds better.

REAL-WORLD SCIENCE!

Scientists try to find out more about what's inside the earth by drilling holes. They take pictures and samples of what they see. By looking at this information, they can determine what the inside of the earth is like. They also measure the waves of energy put out by earthquakes. And they send waves of energy bouncing around inside the earth. No one has actually ever seen a sample from the core, but by taking these measurements, scientists can **theorize** (make an educated guess) about what's in there.

STUFF YOU NEED
- Paper plate (this is going to be sort of like a workstation, so try not to dirty up the place with sand and clay)
- Plastic knife
- 3 colors of clay (ideally, red, orange, and blue)
- Sand or sugar (about 1/2 cup or 120 mL)

1 Using the red clay, **ROLL UP A BALL** about the size of an egg yolk. Eliminate all creases and make the ball as perfectly round as possible.

2 Flatten a piece of orange clay into a pancake shape. Place the red ball on top of the center of the orange pancake. **WRAP THE PANCAKE AROUND THE RED BALL.** Roll this new orange ball around so that it is perfectly symmetrical.

3 **MAKE AN EVEN BIGGER PANCAKE** shape with the blue clay. Wrap that around the orange ball. Roll it around so that it's as close to a perfect ball shape as possible.

4 Roll the whole ball around in the sand or sugar on the plate so that the ball is mostly coated with it. **THIS IS YOUR MINI-EARTH!**

5 **CUT THE EARTH IN HALF!** Actually, just take a knife and slice your clay ball in half.

6 You'll see four layers:
· **RED:** the core
· **ORANGE:** the mantle
· **BLUE:** the crust
· **SAND OR SUGAR:** the top layer of the crust—the earth we stand on.

And here's the amazing part: In all those layers that form the ball that is the Earth, the only part of it where humans can live is the tiny, thin, shaky top layer of crust. **ALL LIFE THAT WE KNOW OF EXISTS ON THE EARTH'S CRUST.**

FACT BOX

Here's how deep scientists think the layers of Earth are. These are averages, as the depths can vary from place to place.

CORE: 2,200 miles (3,540 km) in diameter

MANTLE: 1,300 miles (2,092 km)

CRUST: 3 miles (5 km)

BONUS! BE A GEOLOGIST!

Take a core sample of your mini-Earth. Stick a straw into the ball of clay, all the way to the middle. Then carefully pull it out, trying to keep the clay in the straw. Use a stick to push the clay back out of the straw. See the layers? That's a **core sample**.

NATURAL DISASTERS

SCIENCE ACTIVITY:

Mine for chocolate.

THERE'S GOLD (CHOCOLATE) IN THEM THAR HILLS!

WHY DID THE MINER FLY A BALLOON INTO A THUNDERSTORM? He heard every cloud had a silver lining!

Dig this: We get tons of important minerals from inside the Earth! Miners are people who find and remove minerals from below the planet's surface. Today, they mostly use huge machines to chip away at the ground to bring up diamonds, gold, coal, copper, and more. But back in the olden days (ask your parents if they remember), miners searched for substances like coal and gold by hand. Today, scientists study the land and the rocks to figure out where important minerals are located. Then mining companies dig, dig, dig to get to the treasure.

The minerals they bring up were created over millions of years by pressure and chemistry. Over time, the elements of the Earth formed and reformed to create hundreds of different types of minerals.

Mining is hard and dangerous work. People and machines go deep underground to find the minerals we need for making things like cell phones, foil wrap, car batteries, and even vitamins!

Let's do some mining of our own . . . with a treat at the end!

BIG NUGGET!

The world's biggest nugget was not made of chicken . . . it was made of gold. It was found in Australia in 1869. It weighed 158 pounds (71 kg)!

STUFF YOU NEED
- Plate
- Toothpicks
- Chocolate chip cookie (the bigger, the better!)

STEP by STEP

1 THE CHIPS IN YOUR COOKIE ARE THE MINERALS you have to mine.

2 Start "digging" using your toothpicks. Can you extract (take out) the chips without breaking them? YOU CAN BREAK THE COOKIE!

3 WRITE DOWN ANY CHALLENGES YOU FACE; how do you think those translate to real-world mining? Can you imagine if those chips were diamonds in hard rock?

FUN FACT

The Mponeng gold mine in South Africa is the world's deepest mine. More than 4,000 miners go down (way down!) 2.4 miles (3.9 km) every day to dig for the shiny stuff!

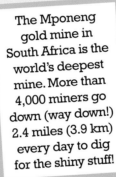

4 Now the best part (and the part that real miners can't do without really hurting their teeth): EAT WHAT YOU DUG UP!

REAL-WORLD SCIENCE!

Did you know that California was pretty much created by mining? In 1848, a man named John Sutter found some gold in a California creek. Word spread quickly. The "gold rush" was on! By 1849, so many people had arrived to search for gold that California became a state! There have been gold rushes in Canada, Australia, New Zealand, South Africa, Brazil, and Peru, too!

Construct a building that can stand up to an earthquake.

EARTH-QUAKE!

STUFF YOU NEED
- Craft sticks
- Clay
- Styrofoam pieces
- Table, like a card table or small dining table
- Newspaper (to protect the tab from the mess!)

Have you ever experienced an earthquake? I hope not—it is pretty frightening. An earthquake is a geological event in which the Earth's crust moves. As it moves, whatever is on top—roads, buildings, people—starts to shake and vibrate. It is scary!

In 2010, there was an earthquake that had a 7.0 **magnitude** (the measurement scientists use to describe the strength of a quake, do you remember this from page 67?) that rocked the Caribbean island of Haiti. The earthquake was so strong that many buildings crumbled like sand. About a month later there was an earthquake in Chile that had a magnitude of 8.8, yet many buildings there survived.

Why do you think that the stronger earthquake in Chile caused less damage to buildings than the weaker earthquake in Haiti? Make some guesses!

Believe it or not, the reason was how the buildings in each place were built. When you construct any structure, you need to take your time and create a great architectural design, but you also have to try to make it strong enough that it stays up in an earthquake. Engineers must use the right materials, the right design, and the right foundations for any building in an area where earthquakes happen. How do you think a building you designed would do in an earthquake? Let's find out!

EARTHQUAKE FACTS

• The Earth's crust is made up of plates, sort of like a jigsaw puzzle. The place where the pieces meet is called a fault. When those edges that lie along a fault move, that's an earthquake, and anything resting on those pieces gets shaken.

• The San Andreas Fault, one of the biggest in the United States, runs right through California. That state has had several very bad earthquakes over the years. One came just as Game 2 of the 1989 World Series was about to start!

• The faults around the Pacific Ocean cause the most earthquakes. Countries including Japan, China, the Philippines, and Indonesia all have to watch out for earthquakes.

1 **GATHER YOUR BUILDING MATERIALS. Using** these materials, you are going to build the tallest structure that you can. You will then test it in your very own earthquake machine.

WHAT DID ONE EARTHQUAKE SAY TO ANOTHER EARTHQUAKE? It's not my fault!

2 Remember, YOUR GOAL IS TO BUILD A STRUCTURE THAT IS STABLE AND CAN RESIST THE FORCE OF GRAVITY AND THE POWER OF THE EARTHQUAKE. You can choose the shape of your structure based on whatever you think is going to be strongest—a cube, a pyramid, a rectangle, whatever— the choice is up to you. Remember, you are the engineer.

3 Once you have determined what shape you want your structure to be, construct a one- or two-story frame structure. USE THE POPSICLE STICKS AS THE "SKELETON" AND THE CLAY FOR THE JOINTS. In other words, the clay should be used to hold the sticks together. If you want, you can use a Styrofoam piece to make a foundation for the building.

4 When your structure is complete, you will TEST IT THROUGH A SERIES OF EVENTS, just as real engineers do.

5 To do this, TAKE OUT YOUR EARTHQUAKE MACHINE. You don't have an earthquake machine in your house? Really? I thought everyone had one. Look around and make sure . . . okay, I'm just kidding around. The earthquake machine is the table on which you built your building! Leave your structure on the table and start thumping on the table with your hands. Keep smacking the table for about 20 seconds. The vibrations from your hands will travel through the table and hit your structure. This is your very own human-made earthquake.

6 WHAT HAPPENED TO YOUR STRUCTURE? Did it fall? Is it leaning? Can you make changes to your structure that will make it stronger? Can you try shaking the table side to side to see what a stronger earthquake would do? What redesigns can you make so that your building (and the people in it) survive? It's up to you!

CONSTRUCTION TIPS

Try cross- or diagonal-bracing to further stabilize your building. Cross-bracing means you put in vertical X-shaped braces between the popsicle stick walls. Try different materials such as craft sticks, kite string, and straws for your crossbraces and see which work best.

NATURAL DISASTERS

73

LOVE THAT LAVA!

WHAT DOES A ROCK WANT TO BE WHEN IT GROWS UP?

A rockstar!

STUFF YOU NEED

- Large cookie sheet or tray to hold the experiment
- 3-ounce (90 mL) paper cup
- Tape
- Styrofoam or heavy paper plate
- Aluminum foil to wrap around plate
- Water
- 1 cup (120 g) of baking soda
- 2 tablespoons (30 mL) white vinegar
- Red food coloring (a few drops for awesome lava effect!)
- Spoon

Rumble, rumble, rumble . . . blam! An erupting volcano is one of nature's most amazing sights. It can also be one of the most dangerous. In an eruption, hot lava, which is **molten** (melted) rock, pours out of the volcano's mouth along with ash, rocks, and a whole lot of smoke. (When a solid gets so hot that it turns into a liquid, it becomes the molten form of that solid.)

In the past, people did not know when a volcano was about to erupt. Today, scientists have instruments that can sense what's going on inside a volcano and give people a better idea of when something is going to happen. They can warn people living nearby when it is safe and when to stay away.

In this experiment, we're going to make a volcano. But don't worry, it won't spread boiling hot lava around your room. It might make a mess, though, so make sure to build it somewhere your parents won't mind!

WHAT DID THE BOY VOLCANO SAY TO THE GIRL VOLCANO?

I lava you!

74

1 Put a rolled-up piece of tape, sticky side out, in the middle of the plate. TAPE THE BOTTOM OF THE CUP TO THE MIDDLE OF THE PLATE.

WHERE DO ROCKS SLEEP? The bedrock!

2 Now COVER THE PLATE AND THE CUP WITH FOIL, leaving some hanging over the bottom. Form the top part of the foil into a cone shape so that it covers the outside of the cup and plate. When it looks like a cone, fold the bottom of the foil under the plate, and pinch it with your fingers around the plate's rim to seal it. You can tape it down if you like.

3 CUT A SMALL X IN THE FOIL over the top of the cup. Carefully push the cut pieces down into the cup so that you have an opening. Pinch the foil around the edges to seal them.

4 PUT TWO TABLESPOONS (30 ML) OF WATER INTO THE BOTTOM OF THE VOLCANO … er, the cup!

5 DISSOLVE A TABLESPOON (15 ML) OF BAKING SODA IN THE WATER. (That means put the soda in and stir it around until it's mixed.)

6 In a separate cup, MEASURE 2 TABLESPOONS (30 ML) OF VINEGAR. Add a drop or two of food coloring for special effects!

7 Now: THE BIG SHOW! Pour the vinegar into the baking soda . . . and watch the lava flow!

NATURAL DISASTERS

DON'T BE IGNEOUS!

Though it sounds like it might be a good insult, the word **igneous** (IG-nee-us) actually describes the rocks that we find on Earth that were made by volcanoes!

REAL-WORLD SCIENCE!

Volcanoes can be dangerous, but they also have good effects. They release pressure from inside the Earth. And the lava forms new land above the sea. The islands of Hawaii, for example, were all formed by volcanoes. In fact, the tallest mountain anywhere on Earth is not Mount Everest. Can you guess? It's Hawaii's Mauna Loa—if you include the parts that are under the sea, it is waaaaay taller than Everest!

TORNADO IN A BOTTLE

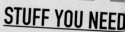

- 2 16-ounce (480 mL) plastic bottles
- Duct tape
- Water
- Glitter, very small beads, or anything tiny enough to fit through the neck of the bottle

Tornadoes are among the scariest and most unpredictable natural weather events. They are formed by huge storms that produce high winds. The winds turn and spin and twist. The tornado happens when the winds twist so fast that they form a certain shape called a **vortex** (VOR-teks) that touches the Earth. When that happens, the winds can tear apart houses and fling cars around like toys.

In this experiment, we're going to form a vortex—a mini-tornado—in a soda bottle. But don't worry, this tornado won't damage your house . . . and you won't be spun into the Land of Oz!

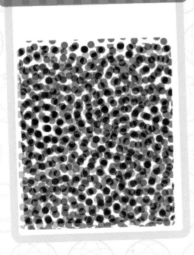

SCIENCE WORD

Vortex: This cone shape is formed when winds whip around and round. Narrow at the bottom and wide at the top, the vortex can become a tornado.

REAL-WORLD SCIENCE!

A tornado is a vortex of air. But they don't just happen on land in storms. A **vortex** from a storm over water forms a huge **waterspout**, pulling seawater into the air. In a raging forest fire, the heated air can create a vortex called a **fire devil** which creates a column of flame! And swirling winds in a desert environment can form a **funnel cloud**.

1 FILL ONE OF YOUR BOTTLES ¾ OF THE WAY WITH WATER. **Add glitter and other tiny, cool things to the water.**

2 TURN THE SECOND BOTTLE (EMPTY!) UPSIDE DOWN **over the first bottle (the one with water in it).**

TORNADO ALLEY

In the Midwestern area of the United States, so many tornadoes happen during summer thunderstorms that parts of Nebraska, Kansas, Oklahoma, and Texas are called "Tornado Alley."

3 Using duct tape, TAPE THE TWO NECKS OF THE BOTTLES TOGETHER. **Make sure that you add enough tape so that the two bottles are bound tightly and do not fall over.**

4 TURN THE TOP BOTTLE OVER **while rotating the bottom bottle clockwise. (Not sure what clockwise is? Look at a clock. What direction are the hands moving? That's clockwise!) As the water travels from one bottle to the other, a vortex will be created and you will have made a tornado in a bottle!**

REAL-WORLD SCIENCE!

Scientists called **storm chasers** go right to the heart of tornadoes. They track the storms and race to those locations with lots of instruments so they can study the winds and forces at work. This is very dangerous, but it can help save lives. If scientists can learn how to predict tornadoes, they can warn people when one is on the way and explain how to take shelter safely.

NATURAL DISASTERS

77

MUDSLIDE!

WHY CAN'T YOU STARVE IN THE DESERT? Because of all the sand which is there.

A mudslide happens when the usually solid ground on a slope or hill becomes so filled with water that it turns into thick, heavy mud. The ground erodes and starts to move, slipping and sliding down the hill, thanks to gravity.

Have you ever seen a mudslide? I bet you have, actually. Have you ever made a sandcastle at the beach? You filled up a bucket with sand, added water, turned it over, and presto—you made a castle out of sand. But eventually a wave came and hit your creation. What happened? The sand in your castle started to topple and slide. So much water hit your castle that the sand just couldn't hold itself together. There is space between the grains of sand, and once that space fills up with water and cannot hold any more water, it comes crashing down. This is how mudslides happen.

For this experiment, a paper plate will be your solid ground—you are going to find out what happens to that ground when it has to hold too much water.

STUFF YOU NEED
- Plate
- Spoon
- Water
- Eyedropper
- Plastic cup
- Toy people
- Sand (enough to fill a beach bucket—you can get it at just about any hardware store)

1 FILL THE PLASTIC CUP WITH SAND. Make sure the cup is filled to the top! There is air between the grains of sand, so you are going to have to press the sand down and get rid of all that air. Once you have done this, add more sand so that the cup is filled to the top. Press it down again and level it off until the cup is filled.

2 Now you have to ADD WATER TO THE CUP OF SAND so that it can keep its shape. You do not want to add too much water or it will be muddy. You do not want to add too little water or it won't hold together when you turn it over.

3 Use a spoon to add water to the cup of the sand. GO SLOWLY SO THAT IT DOESN'T OVERFLOW. You might have to experiment with this a couple of times to get the sand and water mixture just right.

4 TURN THE CUP OVER ON THE PLATE. Tap it lightly and then lift the cup up off the sand pile. You have now made a hillside.

5 Now use YOUR EYEDROPPER TO ADD DROPS OF WATER, one at a time, to the same spot on your hillside. Add 20 drops and make an observation. Add 40 and observe, then 60, then 80. By the 100th drop, does your hillside become a hill-slide? Add another 100 and what do you observe?

NATURAL DISASTERS

Do you think you would want to live in an area where mudslides occur? **Erosion** happens when water and wind eat away at rock and soil. Did this happen to your hillside?

CHAPTER 6

C.S.I. Kids!

CSI stands for **Crime Scene Investigation.** When a crime is commited, science can often be used to help find out what happened! Experts examine the scene of a crime for clues that the bad guys left behind. Those clues might be fingerprints, footprints, or maybe even lip prints! The CSI experts can also find chemicals that can tell them who was on the crime scene and tiny hairs that they can match up to a real person. It's not as glamorous as on TV or in the movies, but CSI experts solve crimes around the world. Science saves the day!

In this chapter, you'll become a member of CSI Kids! Learn how fingerprints are made and lifted ... find out how invisible colors can be revealed ... and how a footprint can help you find a criminal! Chemistry and physics are the most important sciences for a CSI expert. Put them together with the tools of a CSI and it's called **forensic science.**

Many scientists have left their fingerprints (get it?!) on the history of forensic science. Here are some of the most important:

• In 1814, Spanish doctor MATHIEU ORFILA wrote a book about how to detect poisons.

• The French scientist ALPHONSE BERTILLON developed the first crime, scene kit in 1879, with gear to find and preserve evidence.

• The English writer FRANCIS GALTON was the first to write, in 1892, about fingerprints in a way that could be used by CSI experts. (Fingerprints had been known for centuries, but only by this time were they used to identify people.)

• In the late 1890s, Austrian judge HANS GROSS wrote a book that said science should be used to fight crime.

• In 1910, EDMOND LOCARD set up the first crime lab, in Lyon, France.

CRIME SCENE KIT

C.S.I. KIDS

IN THIS CHAPTER:

Make an imprint of your own fingerprint.

MAKING! FINGERPRINTS!

Put down this book! Now, look closely at your fingers.

Wait . . . if you put the book down, then you won't be able to read this sentence. HEY! Pick the book back up!

Okay, now that we're together again . . . hold the book with one hand and examine the fingertips of your other hand. No, not your fingernails . . . the other side. See those tiny ridges and bumps on the top pads of your fingers? Those are your fingerprints. They are unique to you, which means that no one else in the world has exactly the same pattern of lines, ridges, and bumps that you have. When you touch something, you leave behind a fingerprint that shows all those tiny lines. It's a mark that shows who you

are. For people who investigate crimes, like detectives, fingerprints are among the most important tools for solving the mystery of "WHO DID IT?" If an investigator finds a person's fingerprints at a crime scene, that can lead to finding the criminal. Since no two people have the same prints, they can know for sure who was there.

In this chapter, you're going to become a Kid Detective! How? Good question! First, we'll learn a bit about our own fingerprints. Then we'll learn how to find fingerprint clues . . . and start detecting!

The study of fingerprints is called **dactyloscopy.**

REAL-WORLD SCIENCE!

According to pet experts, a dog's nose print is like a person's fingerprints. No two dogs' noses make the same exact print!

1 On the piece of paper, **DRAW A 4-INCH (10-CM) SQUARE.** Color in the square with your pencil. Use the side of the tip of the pencil, not the tip itself (it'll be quicker).

2 **PRESS THE TOP PART OF YOUR INDEX FINGER ONTO THE COLORED-IN SQUARE ON THE PAPER.** Pressing your fingertip onto the paper, gently roll it back and forth several times. When this is done you are going to notice that you have a very dirty finger. This is perfect!

3 Cover that section of your dirty finger with a small piece of tape. **PRESS THE TAPE FIRMLY ONTO YOUR FINGER.** Don't take it on and take it off again—just press once.

4 **PULL THE TAPE OFF OF YOUR FINGER** slowly and place it sticky-side down on a clean sheet of white paper. (Leave the tape is down on the paper, do not lift it up again!) Now make an observation. What do you see? Presto! Your fingerprint is now visible on your paper, ready for investigation. To make a complete set, do the same thing with all your fingers—and don't forget your thumb.

5 When you have completed all of your fingerprints, take a look at the sheet. **DO YOUR FINGERPRINTS HAVE AMAZING PATTERNS?** What do they look like? Some will look like spirals, some liker roller coasters, and some like slides. Observe your fingerprints and see what creative and descriptive names you can come up with for those patterns.

6 If you have time, **TAKE MORE FINGERPRINTS** and see if your parents, friends, or family share any of the patterns you found in your own fingerprints. You can also do palm prints and even toe prints!

C.S.I. KIDS

REAL-WORLD SCIENCE!

Juan Vucetich of Argentina was the first policeman to use fingerprints to solve a crime. In 1892, he caught a murderer by matching her fingerprint.

THAT NAME PRINT

Fingerprints have some amazing patterns. Believe it or not, these patterns have some really cool names, and none of them are very scientific. A fingerprint that looks like a spiral is called a WHORL. A fingerprint that comes in on one side and rises up then comes out the other side is called an ARCH. A fingerprint that comes in on one side and rises up and then comes out the same side that it started is called a LOOP.

LIFTING!
FINGERPRINTS!

Knowing that people leave unique fingerprints behind is one thing. Finding those fingerprints is another. In the last activity, you were able to see your fingerprints using pencil graphite, but if you haven't covered your fingertips in paint or powder, you don't leave behind a visible print. Which means that even though we know they are there, most fingerprints are invisible. Science can help us see them! Crime-scene experts are scientists who use a variety of tools to gather evidence from the place where a crime was committed— including fingerprints. Once they have the fingerprints, they can use them to match the prints to a person. If they already suspect a person of being the culprit, they can discover whether that person's fingerprints were at the scene of the crime!

But if fingerprints are invisible, how are we supposed to see them? Time to become a **forensic scientist** (someone who uses science to reveal evidence of a crime) and find out!

Did you know that your skin makes oil and sweat? It does, and even though you can't always see it, it's there. Every time you touch something with your hands, you leave traces of those substances on the objects you have touched—that's how fingerprints get onto other objects. Let's find out how to find those fingerprints!

STUFF YOU NEED
- Small paintbrush
- Cocoa powder
- Tape
- Paper
- Ceramic plate

COCOA POWDER

1 Rub the fingerprint part of your pointer finger down the side of your nose from the corner of your eye to the tip of your nostril. **THE OIL FROM YOUR FACE IS NOW ON YOUR FINGER.** You can't see it, but trust me, it's there. I know, I know, it's kinda gross but hey, sometimes scientists have to deal with gross stuff!

2 **PRESS YOUR OILY FINGER AGAINST THE CENTER OF THE CERAMIC PLATE. Lift** your finger straight off the plate; don't slide it around or you will smear your print. By placing it at the center of your plate, you will remember where you left your invisible fingerprint.

FUN WITH FINGERPRINTS

Make some fingerprints with an ink pad. Then turn the fingerprints into little drawings of people, animals, or whatever!

3 **DIP YOUR PAINTBRUSH INTO SOME COCOA POWDER. You do not need a** lot of cocoa powder, so shake or tap the extra powder off of the brush.

4 Use the brush to **LIGHTLY "PAINT" THE POWDER OVER THE CENTER OF THE PLATE.** The powder is going to stick to the oil from your nose and finger. A fingerprint is magically (I mean, scientifically) going to appear on the plate!

5 Now **YOU ARE GOING TO "LIFT" IT,** which is what experts say when they take a fingerprint from a surface. You only have one shot at this, so take your time! Take a piece of clear tape, and press the tape firmly against the cocoa–covered fingerprint. Then slowly and carefully peel up the tape. Next, carefully place the piece of tape sticky-side down onto a sheet of paper. You just lifted a fingerprint!

6 Observe the plate. There's nothing there, right? **YOU'RE IN FOR A SURPRISE.**

At a crime scene, fingerprint experts don't actually use cocoa powder to reveal prints. They carry a bunch of special powders with them, called "fingerprint dusts." When they brush those powders over surfaces that they think will have fingerprints on them, it's called "dusting for fingerprints." If the surface is light-colored, they use black dust. When dusting dark surfaces, they use white or tan dusts.

C.S.I. KIDS

85

SCIENCE QUESTION:

Who stole the chocolates?!

(Okay, not really—
the real science question is,
Can you make black ink . . . into a rainbow?)

COLOR MY WORLD

SCIENCE WORD

Paper **chromatography** is a process for separating the hidden parts of something that is fully mixed up, like black ink. In this experiment, the mixture will be separated into its parts.

Would you believe that someone stole a box of chocolates right out of my classroom? Not only did someone steal it, but they left me a note saying "Thanks for the chocolates!" What nerve!

The note contained a clue, however, which I used to find the culprit! When some water dripped onto the note, I made an amazing observation. When the paper absorbed the water, the ink on the paper started to separate into different colors.

I could not believe my eyes! The black ink was actually made up of a combination of other colors. When scientists separate and analyze those colors, it is called **chromatography**.

So how did I solve the crime? I collected all the black pens from the kids in my class and wrote a word with each one of them. I then wet the papers with the words on them to see which pen made the same color patterns as the note I found. Crime solved!

REAL-WORLD SCIENCE!

BLACK LIGHT

In this experiment, we see how the color black can actually be made of other colors. Crime-scene experts also use special lamps called "black lights" that cast **ultraviolet light**. This is light that humans cannot see, but it can show things that are otherwise invisible. If you shine a black light on a surface, all sorts of stuff will appear, from fingerprints to bloodstains.

STUFF YOU NEED
- 5 different black marker-type pens (Not ballpoint! You can use felt, permanent, or dry-erase marker
- Water and cups
- 5 sheets of one-p paper towel
- Straw

ROY G. BIV

STEP by STEP

WHY WERE THE LITTLE INKSPOTS CRYING? Their father was in the pen!

 1 Using the five pens, WRITE "I LOVE SCIENCE!" on five separate sheets of one-ply (one-layer) paper towel. Number the sheets and pens so you know which goes with which.

2 FOLD EACH PIECE OF PAPER TOWEL IN HALF, then in half again. You'll end up with five cone-shaped pieces of paper towel.

3 HOLD THE FIRST CONE-SHAPED PAPER TOWEL IN A CUP OF WATER so that the point of the cone just touches the water. Hold it still and watch what happens as the water begins to flow up the paper.

4 After the water has reached the outer edge of the paper, REMOVE IT FROM THE GLASS, unfold it, and place it on a newspaper to dry. Repeat with the other pieces.

5 Once they have all dried, OBSERVE THE PATTERNS that have formed on the towels.

6 Did any of the black pens reveal other colors? WHAT COLORS DID THEY REVEAL? Did they all have the same patterns? Did some have more?

7 Now, ASK SOMEONE ELSE TO WRITE A NOTE—without you watching—using one of the black pens. Then follow the method above to see if you can figure out which pen was used!

Want to remember the colors of the rainbow in order? Just remember Roy G. Biv! Those letters stand for:

RED ORANGE YELLOW GREEN BLUE INDIGO VIOLET

How many of those colors did you see in the black ink when you used paper chromatography?

PUTTING YOUR FOOT IN IT

C.S.I. KIDS

Crime-scene experts can't always take the footprints they find home. You can't dig up a huge patch of ground if you find tire tracks on it! Instead, they make casts. They use a special quick-drying clay or cement that creates a perfect reverse-image of the imprint. Back in the lab, they can study it carefully to use it as a clue to solve the crime!

You are on your way to becoming a real kid Sherlock Holmes (in case you don't know, he is a famous detective in stories written by Sir Arthur Conan Doyle). Just like a professional detective, you know how to lift fingerprints. You can examine them to see how they are unique. You can "read" the colors hidden in black ink!

Putting on your detective hat, ask yourself a couple of questions: What other kinds of clues do you think people leave behind when committing a crime? Is there one that we haven't mentioned yet?

I'll give you a hint: What did dinosaurs leave, along with fossils, millions of years ago as evidence of their existence? Here's another hint: Dinosaurs were very heavy. What did they leave behind when they walked? Now you can guess what sort of clues we're looking for. That's right: footprints!

FLOUR

I actually like to call them **imprints**. Imprints are any marks that are made by pressure. When you press a finger into a piece of clay, you have made an imprint. When you are leaning on something and it leaves a mark on your skin, it has made an imprint on you!

Sometimes criminals leave footprints or imprints that investigators will use when they are solving the crime. It is actually very easy to take an imprint, using this recipe for a kind of "clay" that you can make with ingredients from your kitchen.

STUFF YOU NEED
- Ruler
- Big mixing bowl
- Wax paper
- 1 cup (250 mL) of used coffee grounds
- 1/2 cup (120 mL) cold coffee
- 1 cup (250 mL) all-purpose flour
- 1/2 cup (120 mL) table salt

WHY DID THE CRIMINAL TAKE A BATH BEFORE THE BANK ROBBERY? He wanted to make a clean get-away!

STEP by STEP

1 In a large mixing bowl, POUR THE COFFEE GROUNDS, COLD COFFEE, FLOUR, AND SALT. Science is messy and messy is fun, so use your hands to mix the ingredients. Make sure to mix everything together so that the goo ends up looking like muddy clay.

2 After covering your table, GRAB A HANDFUL OF THIS MIXTURE and place it on your table. Flatten it into a ½-inch (1.5 cm) block.

3 When this is done, PRESS YOUR HAND FIRMLY INTO THE BLOCK OF CLAY. What happened? The clay took an imprint of your hand!

4 Reshape the clay and TRY MAKING IMPRINTS OF DIFFERENT OBJECTS that are lying around your home: keys, plastic dolls, pencils, or whatever you can find.

5 When you are done experimenting on the table, cover the floor with a rag or old towel. RESHAPE THE CLAY so that it is as large as your foot, and place the block of clay onto the floor. Take off your shoes and socks.

6 STEP ONE FOOT INTO THE CLAY BLOCK, press firmly, then carefully remove your foot. Let the clay harden . . . that might take a few days.

7 CONGRATULATIONS! You have now added the art of taking imprints to your arsenal of crime-solving skills. You are almost a graduate of CSI kids!

THE 3 Rs: REDUCE, REUSE, RECYCLE
You help the environment by reusing materials that you have around your home. Tell your parents that instead of throwing out their old coffee grounds, they can give them to you and you'll reuse them for this activity.

Some people have made casts of huge imprints to try to prove that Bigfoot exists. This mysterious creature has never been photographed, but some people believe it exists, thanks to the footprint clues.

PUCKER UP!

You've seen how fingerprints can identify someone. No two fingerprints are alike. The same is true about your lips! They might look a lot like other people's lips, but they are all different.

So now, my young forensic scientist, you will need a grown-up to help. I'm going to ask you to please find some dark-colored lipstick and put it on OR find a grown-up who wears lipstick and ask them to be a subject in your experiment. (Never borrow lipstick without asking—people are very picky about other people's lips touching their lipstick!) Before you question me, trust me: This is for the love of science. If anyone wonders why a kid is putting on lipstick, just explain that you're doing it for science.

So, back to the lipstick. Choose red, purple, black, dark pink, whatever suits your fancy, but know that the very pale colors won't show up as well when making prints.

STUFF YOU NEED
- Lipstick in a dark color (make sure to check with a parent before borrowing lipstick)
- Mirror
- Paper

There are just five basic lip patterns among all the human beings in the world! Let's look at the different lip patterns below and see if you can identify which lip pattern belongs to you.

DIAMOND GROOVES

LONG VERTICAL GROOVES

SHORT VERTICAL GROOVES

RECTANGULAR GROOVES

BRANCHING GROOVES

STEP by STEP

1 First, COVER BOTH YOUR TOP AND BOTTOM LIPS WITH LIPSTICK. It's easier if you look into a mirror when you do this.

WHAT DID THE DUCK SAY WHEN SHE BOUGHT A LIPSTICK?
Put it on my bill.

2 TAKE A SHEET OF PAPER and fold it in half.

3 Take the folded side of paper and place it gently into your mouth and press your lips tightly onto the paper. Lift your lips. Bingo . . . A PERFECT LIP PRINT!

4 Observe your lip print carefully. YOUR LIP PRINTS ARE UNIQUE, just like your fingerprints. In fact, no one on planet Earth can have either your fingerprints or your lip prints. They belong only to you!

5 EXAMINE YOUR PRINT and look for patterns, lines, or ridges.

6 Can you think of ways in which AN INVESTIGATOR CAN USE LIP PRINTS to solve crimes?

C.S.I. KIDS

BERRY NICE!

People have been coloring their lips for thousands of years. The ancient Egyptians used colorful fruit and plant juices to tint their lips, and then some scientifically minded ancient Egyptian got the bright idea of adding crushed-up insects to get a really red color. What natural ingredients do you think could be used to color lips?

Hey, banana heads!

I mean, hi, diaper pants! No that's not what I meant to say …

Wait, I got it: What's up, fart machines?

Okay, hang on, let me see if I can get this right! What I am trying to say is: Hellooo, scientists!

Do you know the number one reason I love science? It's because I am allowed to be wrong. I mean, think about it: How often do you get to be wrong? In school, say, with math questions, there is one answer—and it is right or wrong. In sports, you either win or lose. But in science, when you are wrong, you actually win. You win the opportunity to figure out for yourself what is really happening, to challenge your mind, and to learn about the world around you in a fun, active way.

The beauty of the scientific process is that there really is no right or wrong. No one will ever make fun of you if you make a "mistake," because there are no mistakes— only opportunities to learn! In fact, whatever answer you come up with, you learn something! For example, in the egg experiment, if your egg dropped like a stone and cracked open, you learned something about gravity, and realized that if you wanted to protect your egg, you had to do something differently next time! When you tried again, and the egg didn't break, you learned something beautiful—from what non-scientists might have called a "mistake." You asked a question, made predictions, tested them, and ultimately came up with some really cool results. That is science!

And now that you have made your way through this book, observing, predicting, and experimenting, you are an official Science Fellow! Congratulations! You have completed an amazing scientific journey. Do you know what my final conclusion is? You are now a scientist; do not let anyone tell you otherwise! Keep on experimenting!

—Carmelo the Science Fellow

"There is no such thing as a failed experiment—only experiments with unexpected outcomes."

—Buckminster Fuller
(American inventor)

"There are no mistakes!"
—Carmelo the Science Fellow
(American scientist)

WATER

VINEGAR

BAKING SODA

A NOTE TO PARENTS AND TEACHERS
ABOUT COMMON CORE AND NEXT GENERATION

As a science teacher, I understand very thoroughly the importance of connecting the experiments in this book to rigorous curriculum standards. There has been a lot of discussion and debate about the introduction of the Common Core State Standards (CCSS), much of it confusing! What do you need to know? The Common Core State Standards were developed for English Language Arts & Literacy and Mathematics. For science standards, the National Research Council, the National Science Teachers Association, the American Association for the Advancement of Science, and Achieve came together to develop the Next Generation Science Standards (NGSS). I have made certain to align each experiment and activity in this book to these standards. For a detailed explanation of how the experiments and activities connect to these standards, please visit my website: carmelothesciencefellow.com, where you can download a document that outlines the connections.

YOUR SCIENCE NOTEBOOK

NOTES

YOUR SCIENCE
NOTEBOOK

INDEX

Carmelo "the Science Fellow" Piazza has been teaching science to Brooklyn elementary school kids for more than 17 years. His signature high-energy, funny, charismatic style made his summer camp and after-school programs tremendously popular, and led him to open the first Brooklyn Preschool of Science, where the science-based curriculum provides a foundation for meaningful language, literacy, and math development. Carmelo lives in Brooklyn with his wife and 4 little scientists.

James Buckley, Jr. is the author of more than 25 books for kids, and has contributed hundreds of articles to dozens of national magazines. Formerly editor of two national children's magazines, Jim was also senior editor with NFL Publishing and editorial projects manager for *Sports Illustrated*. Jim lives in San Diego, CA, with his family.

Chad Geran is an illustrator, husband, father of two little boys, and former sleeper. He lives in Regina, Saskatchewan. He is the author of *Oh, Baby!* (POW!, 2014). Visit Chad at www. geran.ca.